Multiplying disciples of Jesus has been on our minds since 1927. Now in a new century, we've expanded our aims. Sure, we continue to train pastors, but we don't stop there. We equip coaches, counselors, chaplains, missionaries, educators, and lay leaders for a lifetime of effectiveness. For credit, or for enrichment. On campus, or online. And our students count on our ministry-seasoned faculty to deliver high touch, iron-sharpening-iron interaction—the sort that leaves them changed.

So finish reading *Multiply Together*. Then explore how training with us might be a game-changer for your part in building up the Church.

www.westernseminary.edu/why

WESTERN SEMINARY
Gospel-Centered Transformation

GCD BOOKS

Small Town Mission: A Guide for Mission-Driven Communities by Aaron Morrow

The Sermon on the Mount: A 31 Day Guide Through Jesus' Teaching by Tracy Richardson

Sent Together: How the Gospel Sends Leaders to Start Missional Communities by Brad Watson

The Stories We Live: Discovering the True and Better Way of Jesus by Sean Post

Make, Mature, Multiply: Becoming Fully-Formed Disciples of Jesus by Brandon D. Smith

Follow us on Twitter @GCDiscipleship

Purchase at GCDiscipleship.com

MULTIPLY TOGETHER

A Guide to Sending and Coaching
Missional Communities

MULTIPLY
TOGETHER

A Guide to Sending and Coaching
Missional Communities

Brad Watson

ISBN-13: 978-0692784358
ISBN-10: 0692784357

Cover design by Gretchen Jones Watson

— To my fellow pastors and coaches

TABLE OF CONTENTS

APPENDIX OF TOOLS FOR COACHES

INTRODUCTION

What drives the notion and longing for multiplication? My motivation began with the street Mirela and I spent five years living on in southeast Portland. The street where we brought home our first two children from the hospital. The street where we lit firecrackers. The street where we had a parade of costumes during Halloween. The street where we had almost daily gatherings on the sidewalk to tell stories, laugh, cry, and connect. This was the street we also hosted multiple missional communities. This is the street where our neighbors became our friends.

These friends included a fifty year old master craftsman who spent twenty-five years renovating and adding on to his home. He was raised Lutheran but hadn't believed "in that stuff in years." However, he always asked about that "church" that met in our home, adding, "I like that." His wife is a spunky Thai woman who always made us laugh. Together, they own and run one of the best Thai restaurants in the city where they serve traditional dishes from scratch following the recipes of her mother and her homeland.

Our neighbors to our left were a couple who called themselves the "village idiots." He is a Christmas tree farmer, and she is a professor of European history at a local college. We always have great conversations about Christianity, its roots, and its impact on culture. They're also curious about our church, calling it "first century."

Across from us lived a family with two young children. The dad is an architect who dreams of designing sky scrappers but was never given that chance at work no matter how hard he tried. They later moved to San Francisco to chase that dream with a new company.

Next to them was a couple and their son from Boston. The father was a close friend of mine. He had traveled the world before settling down, desperately desiring a life of meaning. He loves live music and golf. We had long conversations about faith, grief, sin, and what makes a person whole. He had two vivid childhood memories. One was of the scolding he received from taking communion incorrectly, and the other was of the day his father died.

Our other friends on the street included a masseuse who spent years in Afghanistan trying to help people before the most recent war. Her partner was an app developer and is one of the funniest people I've ever met.

Another dear friend is an elderly woman who raised a family as a single mom in San Francisco. She is the neighborhood grandmother and lavished my children with gifts, hugs, and encouragement.

Our dearest friends on that street, were our neighbors across the alley. She was a yoga instructor and her husband ran a premier chai company. Their children were named after places from their pilgrimage to Tibet and the Himalayas. We shared many laughs, struggles, doubts, and beliefs.

These were our neighbors and friends. We shared five incredible years together on Southeast 31st Street. Mirela and I were the only family that participated in a church. A few were Christians who had walked away from faith, but most were atheists, agnostics, or "spiritual but not religious." For many, we were the first Christians they had contact with in a long time and we were the only Christians they were friends with. We were some of the few people they knew talking about God, much less Jesus. While they had each encountered the Christian faith in a variety of ways before we moved to the neighborhood, we had the privilege of making the message of Christianity more clear. Over the years and through hosting multiply missional communities, The gospel was clarified.

Our neighborhood had over 180 streets just like this. Our city has over twenty neighborhoods like this. Our country has over fifty urban areas and cities like ours. I write books about missional community with the hope of equipping, igniting, and teaching people to fill those streets, neighborhoods, and cities with missional communities that make the gospel clear to people like my neighbors. While we've seen many communities planted in our city and our neighborhoods, God is not finished in our city.

The vision of missional communities is not simply for one vibrant community but thousands. Thousands of groups reflecting the gospel, growing in the gospel, and proclaiming the gospel to those around them. I pray for thousands of communities speaking the gospel, redeeming culture, and seeking justice in our cities. The vision is faithfulness, obedience, and gospel growth in the lives of ordinary people, doing extraordinary things in the power of the Holy Spirit. The hope is multiplication into every street and every neighborhood. In other words, the prayer is for a movement of gospel demonstration and proclamation.

Previously, I've written to leaders of missional communities (*Sent Together*, 2015) and to missional communities themselves (*Called Together*, 2014). This book is dedicated to those overseeing and equipping leaders to help them in the task of multiplying communities. I took on this book to help us send missional communities to every street, neighborhood, and city. I believe multiplication is the path before us and I believe coaching leaders to live out what they know God has called them to is the structure that enables a thriving, decentralized movement of missional communities.

PART 1:

MULTIPLYING MISSIONAL COMMUNITIES

CHAPTER 1 |

SENDING LEADERS AND MULTIPLYING COMMUNITIES

My wife and I have stepped into the vision of multiplication seven years ago in Portland. We multiplied our own community four times over the first six years. Each time the process was filled with joy and pain. Joy in the excitement of what God was doing and how he was sending people into new corners of the city we love. There was joy in the reality that God would transform the people we sent. There was also pain; knowing community life would never be the same. Change is painful.

The hardest people to send are the leaders we loved and who loved us. We have a special bond with the leaders. We loved alongside them, shared life with them, and shared the responsibility of making disciples with them. Over the last several years, we discovered a new piece of our calling and giftedness: leading and loving leaders. We trained, coached, and released leaders to go and start new gospel families across Portland. The gospel sent them out and they multiplied with our community. This entire book is a testament to the joy and pain of sending and coaching those leaders.

MULTIPLICATION IS HARD AND FRUITFUL

Sending, or multiplication, is one of the sexier parts of gospel communities on mission. Many envision a rapid expansion of the church throughout the globe, but the reality is less sexy. Multiplication is difficult and messy on nearly every level. It takes energy, emotion, and relationship. Ultimately, it means some of your dearest friends and those you have invested in the most leave you for something else. You step into multiplication because the gospel is worth it and Jesus' commands us to go and make disciples.

For all its hardship, the sending of new communities is an incredible apologetic for the gospel to others. As my wife and I multiplied communities, our neighbors got to observe. They saw us send friends to start new communities, serving new neighborhoods, and speaking the gospel in new ways. A neighbor asked me recently about a couple we sent to India, "So they went to India to share the good news? That's such a good thing!" I responded, "Yes, it's completely worth it." (And this neighbor is not a Christian!) Sending new people out means an increase of gospel demonstration and proclamation opportunities.

MULTIPLICATION IS EQUIPPING AND SENDING LEADERS

Multiplying missional communities is actually multiplying leaders. The process of new communities beginning in new neighborhoods begins with two or three leaders with a deep love for Jesus (who he is and what he has done) and a track record of service (people who are already leveraging their lives for others). They are also people who desire leadership and who want to disciple a group of believers into living on mission and in community.

If you talk to these leaders, you will hear the gospel spoken, you will hear a heart for their lost friends, and you will hear a Christ-like love for God's family. Multiplication begins with leadership. As an equipping staff, we spend lots of times with these leaders, mentoring and coaching them in leading a community, praying alongside them, and living on mission with them. Within Bread&Wine, we spend a sizable piece of our budget to train leaders and potential leaders proactively. (More on how create a leadership training process can be found in the appendix).

MULTIPLICATION IS CENTRAL TO BEING A MISSIONAL COMMUNITY

Missional communities are sending agencies into new neighborhoods, cities, and nations. To be clear, it is not that these communities grow in numbers and need to split, or that communities have a polished growth chart. Multiplication is a function of gospel work and empowerment of the Spirit. New communities are sent out of existing gospel communities because the gospel is advancing and sending us into new parts of the world. Simply put, this is what missional communities are.

If multiplication is central to the DNA of a missional community, it is important to remind ourselves of what they are. Missional communities are a way to organize the church to gather and send people on a common mission. Missional communities are a group of people who are learning to follow Jesus together in a way that renews their city, town, village, hamlet, or other space. This renewal and this learning to follow Jesus will innately produce going and sending. Missional communities aren't fancy pyramid schemes. They also aren't perfect groups of people getting copied and pasted throughout cities. In fact, they are pretty messy group of everyday citizens who are devoted to Jesus, to one another, and to their neighbors and city. Gospel-centered communities not only engage mission together, they also engage multiplication together.

Gospel Enjoyment: Growing in Our Love For God Together

Missional Communities answer the discipleship command to grow in their enjoyment of the gospel. As redeemed and adopted sons and daughters of God, we are invited and ushered into a life completed and united to God. God has lavished every spiritual blessing on us; our calling is to receive that love and to love God in return.

Missional communities have the goal of growing in the enjoyment of the gospel together. We grow together through reading the scriptures and practicing confession, repentance,

19

and faith. Communities seek to know God and give him their hearts, minds, and strength. In a missional community, a disciple of Jesus is within a context where the gospel is not only spoken but devoured and ingested into their life. We imagine disciples flourishing in a spiritual life that impacts every aspect of their earthly lives and results in worship and mission.

Community: Growing in Our Love For One Another

Missional communities are also created with the goal that everyone would grow in the aspiration to love one another. We hope to see every missional community centered on God's sacrificial love and marked by extending that love to one another. Missional communities are a discipleship environment where we are challenged to give gifts, time, compassion, and peace to one-another freely. In other words, we grow in all the one-another's of the New Testament:

- Comfort one another (2 Cor. 13:11)
- Agree with one another (2 Cor. 13:11)
- Live in peace with one another (2 Cor. 13:11)
- Greet one another (2 Cor. 13:11)
- Bear one another's burdens—which in context refers to confronting sin and being burdened for the sinful brother (Gal. 6:2)
- Bear with one another (Eph. 4:2)
- Encourage one another (1 Thess. 5:11)
- Build one another up (1 Thess. 5:11)
- Do not grumble against one another (Jas. 5:9)
- Do not speak evil against one another (Jas. 4:11)

Community gets expressed through listening to each other and knowing one-another's stories. We care for the burdens, pains, and struggles each person walks through. We celebrate, and we mourn. Also, we serve each other in our areas of need, whether it is yard-work or babysitting. Ultimately, community is a discipline of sacrifice and giving.

Mission: Growing in Our Love for Our Neighbor Together

Lastly, missional communities are created to pursue mission together. We are called to not only love God and one another, but love our neighbor as we would love ourselves. We are to seek their flourishing. This applies to our wealthy CEO neighbor, refugees down the street in apartment complexes, and the homeless folks who collect our glass for recycling. Missional communities are structured around one common mission where everyone's gifts and capacities work together to share the gospel in word and deed.

Missional communities grow in this area by conspiring to care, learn, show up, and build relationships with those around them. Participating in this common mission reinforces the way we live on mission in the everyday scattered reality of life.

SEEKING GOSPEL GROWTH AND MULTIPLICATION

Each of these goals of a missional community direct us down path to receive, discover, and relearn the gospel. Each teach us the gospel and depict the gospel. As we pursue faithfulness we discover Jesus' right love for the Father and his submission to the Spirit. As we seek to love the community of saints, we are reminded of Christ's incredible sacrifice and love that forms the Church. When we love the poor and vulnerable, we begin to imagine God's great love for the world.

Missional communities are the garden plot of this sort of growth and transformation. We cannot guarantee the formation of disciples of Jesus, but we can make the gospel central and expect fruit. We can expect a deeper awareness and trust in God. We can expect a growing sacrificial love for others over time. We can expect people to respond to the confrontation and challenge of the gospel. We can pray these expectations and hope to see disciples grow up into maturity because of the gospel. I'm confident we will discover potential leaders and see multiplication as we persevere in the gospel. The following chapters offer a biblical and theological framework for why and how missional communities multiply while offering wisdom and insight into leading community through sending.

WORKING IT OUT IN YOUR CONTEXT

- How would you describe your missional communities? How are they living the three aspects of loving God, loving one-another, and loving neighbor?
- How has multiplication been difficult for you? How have you seen it done well?
- What specific challenges do you face with multiplication in your context and church?

CHAPTER 2 |

CREATING A MULTIPLYING CULTURE: LESSONS FROM THE EARLY CHURCH

You can't force multiplication to happen, but you can cultivate an environment where multiplication can happen. As a leader, you can create a culture where sending people is expected, celebrated, and shared by the entire community. There are five important principles from the story of the Church in Antioch and the sending of Paul and Barnabas in Acts. Their story is not merely a pattern to follow but the essence of a multiplying culture. In this chapter, we will unpack these crucial characteristics of communities that send leaders and multiply.

#1: START WITH THRIVING COMMUNITIES THAT MAKE DISCIPLES

The sending out of Paul and Barnabas from the church of Antioch doesn't begin with the prayer meeting in Acts 13 but from the church's inception. The story of the church of Antioch's birth is found in Acts 11:19-26.

> Now those who were scattered because of the persecution that arose over Stephen traveled as far as Phoenicia and Cyprus and Antioch, speaking the word to no one except Jews. 20 But there were some of them, men of Cyprus and Cyrene, who on coming to Antioch spoke to the Hellenists also, preaching the Lord Jesus. 21 And the hand of the Lord was with them, and a great number who believed turned to the Lord. 22 The report of this came to the ears of the church in Jerusalem, and they sent Barnabas to Antioch. 23 When he

came and saw the grace of God, he was glad, and he exhorted them all to remain faithful to the Lord with steadfast purpose, 24 for he was a good man, full of the Holy Spirit and of faith. And a great many people were added to the Lord. 25 So Barnabas went to Tarsus to look for Saul, 26 and when he had found him, he brought him to Antioch. For a whole year they met with the church and taught a great many people. And in Antioch the disciples were first called Christians.

Antioch begins as a church formed out of the ashes of persecution and the proclamation of the gospel from a few faithful people. They proclaimed that Jesus was Lord and many came to believe. They relied on the Holy Spirit, they were generous, and they welcomed help for the formation of this church.

Paul and Barnabas were first sent to Antioch because it was the frontier of mission and the newest church. They were sent to lay a foundation of the gospel, to bless this church, and to encourage them to remain faithful and to walk in obedience to the teachings of Jesus. Many people believed the gospel and became disciples of Jesus. As the church became rooted and thriving in the Holy Spirit, they morphed from being the outskirts to being the launchpad.

This story is not written as a bizarre one-off tale, it's actually describing the ordinary movement of the gospel. The gospel that forms you is the same gospel that will propel you to send. This story in Acts describes the reality that people in your own community will eventually leave to start a new work in another part of the city, another city altogether, or even another country and culture entirely. Sending is a function of gospel growth and maturity. Multiplication happens when disciples are being made, the gospel is being proclaimed, and people are growing in faith.

The foundational assumption of this book is: when you disciple leaders, the effects reverberate through our cities as the gospel is believed, shared, and demonstrated through thoughtful engagement in making and redeeming culture. People following Jesus lead others to follow Jesus, which leads to the sending of others to start communities. Multiplication begins with planting thriving missional communities that are centered on the gospel and faithful to pursue obedience. The church in Antioch was first and foremost an outpost of the kingdom of God and a gospel centered people. If you want to see multiplication happen, invest in laying the foundation. Begin with healthy missional communities.

#2: EXPECT TO PARTICIPATE AND SEND GLOBALLY

The church of Antioch expected the Holy Spirit to advance the good news of Jesus beyond them and to use them. In fact, they had already given of themselves for people beyond themselves in chapter 11.

> *Now in these days prophets came down from Jerusalem to Antioch. 28 And one of them named Agabus stood up and foretold by the Spirit that there would be a great famine over all the world (this took place in the days of Claudius). 29 So the disciples determined, every one according to his ability, to send relief to the brothers living in Judea. 30 And they did so, sending it to the elders by the hand of Barnabas and Saul.*

Before they considered sending a team of people to share the gospel, they had already given their wages, property, storehouses, and food for the well being of people they did not know. They saw themselves as participants in a global kingdom and church, not an isolated one within their own neighborhood. They observed need and determined, as a whole, to send relief for that need. They were a sending church before they sent Barnabas and Paul.

Your community becomes a sending community long before it multiplies. A community that is aware of the hardships of other communities and takes initiative to serve them is preparing itself to send people. A community that is connected to others and not consumed by its own needs is fertile soil for multiplication.

Tips:

- Spend time praying for other missional communities.
- Ask other missional communities if they have any needs and relieve those needs as you have ability.
- Engage in a church overseas, learning their obstacles, praying for them, and giving financially as a whole community.
- Volunteer to help with childcare of one community as a blessing.
- Write encouraging notes and prayers to other communities.

#3: PRAYING, WORSHIPING, AND FASTING IS THE FUEL FOR SENDING

We often think we must talk sending up and discuss it often to make it happen. We believe we can speak multiplication into reality. But, only God speaks anything into reality. God sends while we pray, worship, and fast. God sends while we respond to what he has spoken. Worship is the "vision cast" of mission. You aren't called to spread "vision"; you are called to worship, pray, and fast in light of God's vision for the world. This is an inescapable reality in the book of Acts: Mission occurs in the midst of worship. Mission happens because of worship. Mission results in worship. The elders of Antioch demonstrate this reality well in Acts 13 when Paul and Barnabas are sent in the midst of worship and fasting:

Now there were in the church at Antioch prophets and teachers, Barnabas, Simeon who was called Niger, Lucius of Cyrene, Manaen a lifelong friend of Herod the tetrarch, and Saul. While they were worshiping the Lord and fasting, the Holy Spirit said, "Set apart for me Barnabas and Saul for the work to which I have called them." Then after fasting and praying they laid their hands on them and sent them off. So, being sent out by the Holy Spirit, they went down to Seleucia, and from there they sailed to Cyprus. – Acts 13:1-4

The Holy Spirit sent them while they worshiped Jesus as Lord. A community that sends will be one that is regularly praying and worshiping God. Furthermore, that community will be listening to the voice of God with a dependence on him, knowing the Spirit will send.

Worship dependent mission reproduces enjoyment of the gospel. Worship fueled mission reproduces humility and dependence on the Holy Spirit. Worship inspired sending beckons everyone to listen to the Holy Spirit for what they are being called to. It is through gospel enjoyment that we plant the seeds of multiplication and create a culture that sends. We are turning our hearts and minds to Jesus, the king of his kingdom, the author and actor of the gospel. In this posture, we come to multiplication with humility, awe, trust, and joy. The scope of the gospel is on display and the scope of mission becomes clear. We cannot cast a vision better than a God who sent himself to love others and make the world whole. Worship dependent mission creates the expectation that God will send us to the whole world.

Tips:

- Regularly participate in a worship gathering! Worship is song, prayer, learning, giving, and communion with other saints. Communities that don't make this a regular rhythm almost never multiply.
- Spend time as a community intentionally fasting and praying for the gospel to bear fruit in your lives and beyond your local mission.
- Set aside seasons of prayer and fasting for direction; listening to the Spirit and what he is calling the community to do. This can be an annual rhythm leading up to a new missional commitment. (See appendix)
- Have regular times of gospel enjoyment within your community to learn how to pray, listen, confess, repent, and worship.

#4: PREPARE AND PLAN TO SEND YOUR BEST

In Acts 13, we can see the church and its leaders expecting to send not only their possessions but also their people. They even, you might suppose, expected to send some of the most influential people within the church. Paul and Barnabas spent a year investing in this church and were truly gifted in discipleship, pastoring, and preaching the gospel. We understand from the context of this passage that any of the strong and diverse leaders from Antioch were on the table for the expansion of the mission. They prayed, fasted, and worshipped, and it became evident that Paul and Barnabas were to be sent. But the church was willing to send any or all of their leaders.

Paul and Barnabas had been prepared for a long time. Barnabas was an initial disciple in the church of Jerusalem. He helped establish the church in Antioch and was a spokesman proclaiming what God was doing outside of Jerusalem. His name is actually a nickname, "Son of Encouragement." Every mentioning of Barnabas to this point in Acts has been in connection with serving the church, loving the church, and going outward. It isn't surprising God sends Barnabas, in fact it seems obvious. Paul, on the other hand, seemed destined to go to the western borders of the Empire. Upon conversion, he knew he was saved to preach the gospel to the Gentiles. He knew he would stand before rulers. Everyone knew he would. Despite a few nervous moments in the beginning, the church as a whole had committed to discipling, training, and nurturing Paul in his calling.

The two of them had been prepared by God for this moment through the circumstances of their lives, their churches, and their experience of serving others. They had been taught the gospel, and they had taught the gospel. They had been cared for by the church, and they had cared for the church. The church of Antioch had welcomed them, learned from them, and loved them. Paul and Barnabas grew in Antioch, and they also helped others grow. Though Barnabas arrived at a young church without leaders, he left with increased leadership and maturity.

Leaders are called, developed, and trained within community and by the Spirit. As you establish a missional community, you will prepare and plan to send your best. Instead of keeping the more mature, bought in, equipped, and enjoyable people off limits, prepare them to start new communities. Spend intentional time getting them ready to lead a community. We see this evident throughout the New Testament, as communities freely give great leaders to the mission instead of hoarding them.

Missional communities are simultaneously environments for discipleship and training leaders how to make disciples. This is the chaos and brilliance of communities making disciples. As you go, you prepare others to send. We ought to be constantly looking for the next leaders to develop. Multiplication might happen by sending out first-time leaders, or it may be veteran leaders leaving to start a new community. Regardless, we always develop leaders.

Tips:

- As leaders, pray for who God might send. Pray for opportunities and pray for clarity.
- Look for apprentice leaders you can give opportunities to and make personal development plans with them. (See appendix)
- Help people understand their gifts and affirm one another in their gifts. How do they strengthen the community? How do they help the community on mission?
- Foster growth by having trainings or having other leaders visit to develop everyone.

#5: THE COMMUNITY GIVES ITSELF. IT IS NEVER THE SAME

Lastly, we see the principle of sacrifice in multiplication. Through prayer, grief, and anticipation that God will advance the gospel, the community sends people. To send, God works in the heart of a community to trust in him. To trust that he will give your community everything it needs. The people God gives you are the people God wants you to have. You must trust God's goodness, grace, and ability to orchestrate his mission better than you can.

Multiplication is a sacrifice because the community will never be the same. You cannot replicate what was because the personalities, gifts, and perspectives of the community have changed. As people are sent, what remains is not an old community and new one but two new communities. One is sent out discovering how to be a community of disciples in a new mission or with a new group of people. The other remains and is rediscovering how to be a community that is on mission in the same place and with some of the same people.

This is multiplication. In the last loving act of being a community, it choses to give itself up and never be the same again. For the sake of obedience. For the sake of gospel growth. For the love they have for others who will enjoy a new endeavor of faithfulness. But, also, they multiply for themselves as they experience the new thing God has called them to in their current place and within their current mission. Multiplication is final communal discipline. In Acts 13, this is expressed by praying for them as they go. It's a touching moment of a new reality for both groups of people.

Tips:

- When a plan of multiplication begins to take shape, invite the group to a time of prayer and reflection on what that would mean.
- Give potential leaders clarity on what leadership means and challenge them to step into a process of preparation.
- Celebrate the reality and group dynamics of a community in the present so you can embrace the change when it happens.

WORKING IT OUT IN YOUR OWN CONTEXT

- What can you do today to be the kind of community that multiplies?
- How do you care for communities, neighborhoods, or cities outside your own?
- How do you worship, pray, and enjoy the gospel in such a way as pointing to God's grand global mission?
- How do you develop leaders who listen to the voice of God to send?

CHAPTER 3 |

MULTIPLICATION IS SENDING ARITHMETIC

What are the actual mechanics and skills involved in multiplying communities? How do you send effectively, pastorally, and practically?

There is a simple equation that brings so many questions into focus. It also helps us think through the strategy, process, and prerequisites for a multiplication to happen. This is our multiplication math:

> **Equipped Leaders + Committed Community + Common Mission = New Communities**

Multiplication happens when new leaders are equipped, *and* there's a group or community to lead, *and* there's a mission to engage in. These are the crucial components of a missional community, and they're required to see new communities form. When a multiplication is missing one of these aspects, it doesn't produce new communities, it likely produces crowd management, lone rangers, or pyramid schemes.

COMMUNITY + MISSION - NEW LEADERS = CROWD MANAGEMENT

Sometimes, a community comes to the point where they don't have enough space for everyone in a living room or back yard. There simply isn't room. Getting the community together becomes increasingly difficult. People begin falling through the cracks. I've often experienced communities growing so large that service and engagement in mission actually decreases. No longer do people feel useful and essential; they assume someone else will do what needs to be done. This is a very difficult spot to be in.

Leaders typically get frustrated by the simultaneous size increase and service decrease. Very quickly the leaders might say: "We're too big. We need to multiply." Without new qualified leaders, who have been nurtured and developed, the community often decides to form two communities with the leaders it has. The decision isn't sending out new leaders to be a new missional community; it is splitting the current leadership team.

The communities might move forward for a while before burnout begins to set in for the newly split leaders, but it always comes. They can't carry the load and others don't seem to be stepping up. They are trying to model healthy community, but they're alone in doing it. Often, the leaders quickly realize that of the thirty people in the original community, only ten were truly committed. Those ten were modeling community and speaking the gospel and living on mission together in such a way that others were attracted to it. The original community had a good thing going. However, after the split, that vitality waned. It wasn't multiplication; it was division.

Multiplication Requires New Leaders

Every thriving missional community is led by a team of leaders with unique gifts and perspectives. Multiplication happens when a new team of qualified leaders is equipped and called to form a new community on mission. This is the long and hard work of discipleship. However, it is worth it. Instead of splitting disciples, we multiply disciples!

Leaders are people who will take initiative for the growth, development, and health of a missional community. Leaders function as gardeners, cultivating a discipleship environment. They also live as examples, demonstrating a humble life of repentance, faith, and obedience. Lastly, leaders operate as catalysts who spark conversation and movement toward gospel understanding and mission. Every missional community needs to be led by a team of called, qualified, and equipped leaders. Included in the appendix is more on the qualifications, roles, and callings of leaders into missional communities. Leaders are crucial to missional community life. Multiplication cannot happen without first multiplying leaders.

Returning to the large missional community scenario, imagine what would have happened if, instead of saying: "We're too big, we need to multiply!" they asked these questions:

- What people do we need to invest in more?
- What potential leaders are among us?
- How can we develop people to send?
- How can we as leaders pray for God to multiply our community?

NEW LEADERS + MISSION - COMMUNITY = LONE RANGER

There are also moments when a community has a wealth of leaders being developed with the desire to go and start something new. A few might even sense a true burden for a neighborhood or a people who need the gospel. They can't wait to engage the mission they've been equipped to serve. However, for a multitude of reasons, there aren't people to join them in this mission. The missional community, not wanting to tap the breaks on the leaders' calling, send a few leaders out to the new mission without a core group of people to support and engage the mission as a community.

The result is not a new community but a "lone ranger" struggling to demonstrate Jesus' love. The few leaders burnout as they try to welcome neighbors into a community that doesn't exist. They grow exhausted trying to articulate the gospel without hearing it from another person. The leaders need a community to lead into mission. In the end, the leaders discover this wasn't a multiplication—it was a mission to Mars: send a few people into outer space hoping it works out.

Multiplication Requires a Community

35

It doesn't matter how incredible a leader is, it takes a community to be a missional community. Internally, we realize every missional community needs three to four leaders and six to eight committed adults.

Returning to our lone ranger story, imagine if the leaders saw the genuine excitement of the new leader and lovingly asked them to stay while actively praying for God to send people to join them. The questions they might ask are:

- How can we invite more people into this new community?
- How can we pray for this mission and God to add to the core?
- How can we invest our resources and time into this emerging mission while we wait for people to join it?

NEW LEADERS + COMMUNITY - MISSION = PYRAMID SCHEME

"It's really simple," your friend tells you. "I'll train you and give you everything you need to know, then you go get ten people to train, and they go out and get ten people and so on." This can be called exponential growth or outside church planting circles: a pyramid scheme. The reality is you can do this sort of fast tracked leadership development and multiplication without making disciples and loving neighbors. In fact, communities can perpetually grow, "multiply," and succeed for years without constantly engaging the world around them.

This type of multiplication can be the fool's gold as a metric for success. Communities continue to increase without the gospel advancing beyond our walls and without the poor knowing God's love. Instead of advancing the gospel through community, the gospel is kept in a safe environment for Christians to join.

Multiplication Requires Mission

Missional communities are not a church growth strategy. Missional communities are centered on the gospel and for God's mission to redeem and restore the world. They begin with a common mission in the world. A common mission is the community's unified effort to love—through word and deed—a specific group of people. There are three broad categories for common missions: geography, network, and people.

As leaders are developed and communities are prepared to be sent out the important questions to ask are:

- What is the common mission?
- How will this new community make the gospel clear to those who don't believe?
- How will they share and grow together in loving their neighbors?

MULTIPLICATION RESULTS IN STORIES NOT MATH

Starting and sending new communities is not simply math; it's stories and people. The stories of God moving to gather, send, and bring his kingdom into our hearts and our cities is the phenomenal narrative we are all privileged to live in. While we can get trapped within the math, the stories of God's mission can give us freedom to step into the unknown.

WORKING IT OUT IN YOUR CONTEXT

- What "formula" have you followed in the past? What were the results?
- What motivates multiplication in your context?
- Is there a consistent component missing (i.e., leaders, community, mission)? What can be done structurally to provide opportunities for this?

CHAPTER 4 |

HOW TO LEAD MULTIPLICATION

The process of multiplication can feel like a minefield of expectations, sadness, and miscommunication. It can also feel like something that needs to be orchestrated like a savvy conductor. While there are things to be cautious about, multiplication can be one of the more meaningful and inspiring moments of spiritual growth in a community. In this chapter we will walk through the practical steps and questions to consider as you multiply.

SHARE THE BURDEN AND JOY OF SENDING
One of the biggest mistakes made during a missional community multiplication is keeping the discussions, prayers, and plans private from the group. This is a mistake for variety of relational reasons; however, the biggest is the stealing of participation in what God must be doing. A community's multiplication ought to be shared by the whole group.

Multiplication is a communal discipline facilitated and shepherded by the leaders. The leaders take initiative in supporting and training leaders. Also, leaders bring up the reality of gospel expansion, sending, and care for the mission beyond their view. They build a culture of multiplication and then help the community realize and move toward that as the Holy Spirit leads.

Talk about the multiplication process openly with your community as early as you can. In many ways, the duty of leading multiplication can be best described as: defining and clarifying reality. As a leader, you will regularly discuss the reality of God's mission and the nature of sending, even when multiplication isn't imminent.

Talk like a family. I remember being twelve years old when my father and mother began talking about my brothers and me growing up, graduating high school, and leaving the house. Not only would we leave the house, we would likely leave the country. When we inched closer to my older brother taking the plunge of moving to the States, we talked about it more often. Knowing our family wouldn't be the same, we cried about it more often and we cherished the time we still had together. We began to plan for how we would send him off, and we made a plan for life after his move (including who got his room). When we finally walked him to the passport line at the airport, we were sad but ready to send him on his great adventure. This is how multiplication is done as a family. As a leader, create space for everyone to pray, process, and participate in multiplication.

Pray: Depend on the Spirit to Send

Don't multiply out of compulsion or strategy but multiply together with dependence on the Holy Spirit. Wait for God's timing. It is easy to make decisions to multiply based on numbers, house size, geographic strategy, or out of an urgency to "make something happen." We've tried all of that, and in the long-term it doesn't work out.

Remember the story of Paul and Barnabas at the Antioch Church? Paul had been given the mission of proclaiming the gospel across Europe from the moment of his conversion, then he spent years preparing and waiting for the Spirit to send him out. Their multiplying moment came from a dependence on God and was anticipated for years: "So, being sent out by the Holy Spirit, they went down to Seleucia, and from there they sailed to Cyprus." This is so much better than, "So, being strategic, planned, and fully funded by leaders, they went down to Seleucia, and from there they sailed to Cyprus." We wait and depend on the Spirit together.

I will never forget the evening when our dear friends Joshon and Taylor Miller came over to tell us they had to start a new gospel community. They were compelled by the Spirit to

40

lead a group of their neighbors and friends. This had been the plan from the beginning when they moved to Portland to start a community with us. We knew that one day they would be sent. We waited for the right time in prayer and thoughtfulness, always knowing we would know the time. When they told us their plans and what they felt it looked like to be obedient to God's call, we affirmed it. Our community laid hands on them and sent them out. God's timing was perfect. Our entire community got to play a role in what God was doing, not what we as leaders were orchestrating.

Process: Grieve and Celebrate the Gospel Movement Together

As your community approaches multiplication, bring everyone into a moment of reflection. When we first began sending new leaders out to start new communities, we focused only on the positives: "Look at what God is doing." We would say, "Lets all be happy and throw a big party because we are sending people out!" All of this is true and must be celebrated. We must throw parties, lay hands on those being sent, and trust that God is faithful to sustain his mission. However, something real is lost in sending. Relationships no longer exist in the same way they did previously as people live out their faith in a new place and with new people. The people that go out are leaving something healthy. It is worth acknowledging this relational separation and to remember what was great about being a community.

The best way to process together is to walk through times of reflection on the past and future. Pause and celebrate all God has done in your lives as a community.

- How was the gospel made more clear?
- How did you grow?
- How were you challenged and what memories will you cherish?
- What evidence do we see of God's grace and the Holy Spirit's work?

41

It's also important to look forward with anticipation and allow space for grief. Consider what God is calling you to and what the cost of that calling is.

- What are we excited about in the coming season?
- How is multiplication going to challenge us to trust and obey Jesus?
- What do we hope to see God do in the future with the people in this community?
- What will we miss about this group?

Think of a way to make this time special and unique. While not essential, it can be beneficial to have a weekend away as a community to do this time of processing and reflecting. During one of our most enjoyable multiplications, our entire community of twenty-five people rented a large house on the beach and spent the weekend hanging out and having these sorts of conversations. More than a sweet time, it was a moment that made our multiplication communal.

Also, it isn't a good idea to squeeze this reflection into your last time together. To do this grieving and celebrating well, people need time to share without feeling the rush of another agenda item to accomplish.

Participate: Have a Sending "Event"

You also multiply together by having a clear moment of sending, prayer, and celebration. We often think of it like a birthday celebration, which is pretty accurate. It's also like the christening of a ship set to embark on a maiden voyage. The celebration doesn't make the voyage happen, but it helps everyone involved know it's about to start.

In this sending event, we gather people together one last time to have a feast enjoying the abundance God has already provided and done in the gospel. In this way, we express our joy in participating in his work in the world. As a community multiplies, we humble ourselves in prayer, reminding each other we are not in charge of *his* mission and that the sending is an attempt to follow *him*. We lay hands on those we are sending out and pray for them, knowing it is only the power of God to send ordinary people and birth new thing. This is the capstone moment for your community.

MAKE A PLAN (WITH DATES)

There is a wise saying: "If you don't plan it, it won't happen." Creating a plan with purposeful dates shepherds and cares for your community through what will feel like uncertainty. When it becomes clear that there are leaders, a mission, and a core community ready to be sent, it is time to make a plan for multiplication. No longer is it a theory; you are preparing to launch. Much of the leadership required at this point is to set dates.

Something to consider is the season and the timing. Right before holidays or extended times of vacation, like December and summertime, often make it difficult for communities to gain momentum after a multiplication. However, at the onset of the new year and completion of summer can be great. You have to know your group and the mission, but consider the timing.

Consider all the conversations that must be had to send the new community well and plan accordingly, giving times and responsibilities to everyone. You need to plan:

- A time when the leaders being sent can share the vision for multiplication and invite prayers and thoughts.
- A conversation around the details of a plan and when the multiplication will actually take place.
- A time to celebrate what God has done and will do and to grieve what will be missed.
- A time to pray, launch, and send people out.
- A start day when the groups will be officially multiplied.

ENGAGE IN MUTUAL SUPPORT

Multiplication is not the end of the story but the beginning. As your community continues to multiply the bonds of relationship and shared vision grows, you do not multiply into silos but into the same mission of God and *his* church. New communities are sent together and are forever linked.

Early on, we didn't give much thought to the "post-multiplication" phase. However, once we did we saw remarkable fruit through the support new communities offered each other. As we multiplied, we began thinking about how we support each other afterwards. We began to ask: How will we connect relationally? How can we share mission together? How can we pray for one another? How will we learn from each other?

There are a multitude of expressions of this sort of support:

- Get back together to hang out and hear updates on what is happening in the new missional communities. Meeting quarterly seems to work for many communities.
- Choose to share holiday meals as an "extended family" like Thanksgiving, Christmas Eve, New Years, Easter, the fourth of July, etc.
- Commit to praying for the other community monthly and putting someone in charge of gathering prayer requests.
- Plan several large opportunities to serve the same mission together.

As you can see, multiplication within a missional community perpetuates multiplication and many of the principles discussed in the previous chapters. As communities support and grow in awareness of the other, seeds of multiplication are replanted. When communities multiply more people are equipped as leaders, more people are exposed to the mission of making disciples, and more neighborhoods and streets experience the gospel. Missional communities cease to be a small group strategy and become a movement of the gospel.

THE ONGOING BUILDING OF THE MISSIONAL CHURCH

Coaching is essential for a sustained missional community movement. If you are committed to multiplying discipleship, you must make ongoing investments in the leaders of communities. We call this investment *coaching*. The most significant outlier between effective missional communities and ineffective missional communities is the support and ongoing development leaders receive.

Leaders who do not receive ongoing coaching falter in clarity, gospel fluency, vision, and suffer from isolation. Disconnected and un-coached leaders miss out on the opportunity for leadership to be a journey of growing up in the gospel. Without coaching, leading a missional community becomes a thing to manage.

Coaching leaders happens in the background by discipling with open-ended questions, accountability, encouragement, availability, and friendship. Healthy multiplication happens when the gospel sends some leaders to start new communities and other leaders support and coach them. Multiplication is not an effort done by one person or even one isolated missional community leader, but it is done alongside the care, support, and structure of coaching. We multiply together.

WORKING IT OUT IN YOUR CONTEXT

- How have multiplications been led in the past in your context? What was good and/or bad about that approach?
- Where have communities gotten stuck in their multiplication process? What can prepare leaders to multiply better?
- Which step or suggestion, in this chapter, is a must to implement in your church?

45

PART 2:

COACHING LEADERS AND SUPPORTING COMMUNITIES

CHAPTER 5 |

WHY MISSIONAL COACHING

Coaching is essential for a sustained missional community movement. If you are committed to decentralized discipleship, you must make ongoing investments in leaders. We call this coaching.

TRAINING HAS LIMITS

Classroom equipping and observation can only take you so far. Eventually, leaders have to start taking steps to lead away from the training ground. As they do this, they need accountability, encouragement, and equipping around real scenarios when they are in positions of responsibility and servant leadership.

I will never forget when our community sent Kory and Emily Oman out to start a new community in their neighborhood. The Omans were incredibly equipped through extensive experience and education. They had been to seminary, conferences, and read stacks of books on missional living. Furthermore, they experienced life on mission overseas and within our community for over year. They were prepared to lead. However, our conversations took on a whole new dynamic when they began to lead. We weren't talking theory anymore. There were no hypotheticals. They had real people with real stories and real challenges to discuss when they came to coaching sessions. Kory and Emily didn't have to think about praying and following the Spirit; they actually had to do it. It was in this environment that they began to listen and obey like never before and they learned to pray all over again.

They began throwing the books out the window. Their lives became messy as disciples came into their midst with issues.

Their community ended up looking nothing like the ideal or any other missional community Bread&Wine ever had before. Their core consisted of families scattered across the suburbs. Their neighborhood and community wasn't walkable. Their neighbors didn't value BBQs, art camps, or any other previous strategies our community tried. Kory had to work nights four days a week. Yet, they took steps forward. They opened themselves up to the possibility of failure. They tried different things and prayed prayers like: "Help us be the church here . . . we want to be the church." In the end, through prayer, patience, and listening to the Spirit, they established a thriving family of servant missionaries that cared for homeless teenage moms, foster babies, and they helped each other speak the gospel to their kids. They became a diverse community, declaring the gospel, and demonstrating it on the outskirts of the city. Their lives became immersed in the needs, pains, and blessings of community. They got started with books but moved forward through prayer, faithfulness, and processing with coaches. Coaching bridges the gap between books and real life.

EVERY MISSIONAL COMMUNITY AND LEADER IS DIFFERENT

Communities are not carbon copies. Every community is different because every neighborhood is unique, every group of people is unique, and every mission is unique. Each city has different idols, culture, and barriers to the gospel. The relational dynamics within each small community is special. Each missional community's shared mission brings unique obstacles and opportunities for the gospel. In other words, disciple making is not a reproducible formula or recipe. Forming and developing a discipleship environment like a missional community is very different from making a cake. Primers, books, and curriculum are all helpful in getting you started and laying a solid foundation, but you can't just follow instructions. You simply can't write a step-by-step guide and hand it to people.

Why? This is real life, with real people. The challenges, opportunities, and growth curve for every group of people is different. Furthermore, each leader is uniquely gifted and called. Missional coaches come alongside leaders to be a sounding board, source of gospel truth, partner, and real-time advocate for your missional community. That means a coaching relationship enables the leader to stay focused and follow the leading of the Holy Spirit forward through its dynamic hurdles and calling. Coaches help leaders discover and take the next step in faithfulness. Coaches ask leaders: What does God want us to do now? Coaching is a relationship where unique next steps are discovered and followed.

LEADERS NEED TO BE REMINDED OF THE GOSPEL
Kory and Emily experienced barrier after barrier like all missional community leaders. Our job as coaches was to remind them of the gospel. Coachers are a voice calling leaders to remember who they are, what they are called to, and how discipleship is an act of endurance. As a coach, I spend a large portion of my conversations with leaders reminding them of Jesus, who they are in Christ, and what it means to be a leader of disciples. In the chaos and mess of community, mission, work, and family it is easy to forget where you are and what you are doing. It is also easy to forget what is in your control and what is not. This is why some coaches feel their primary role is to remind leaders of their own calling and its limitations. Coaches ask the questions: Who does God say you are? Why are you doing this? What is true about God in your current situation?

LEADERS NEED TO KNOW THEY AREN'T ALONE
Leadership is lonely. While everyone shares the calling to be discipled and to make disciples, the leaders of communities carry a unique burden of shepherding, encouraging, and facilitating growth in the gospel. This often leads leaders to feel isolated. It is easy for them to forget they belong to a whole, and they are loved. It is even easier to believe they are the only ones that care.

Coaches meet with leaders, in part, to let them know they are not alone. Within the coaching relationship leaders are supported, cared for, and experience friendship. In a coaching relationship, leaders learn that someone else cares about these disciples, and prays for them. Without coaching, leaders experience burnout as they carry increasing burdens on their own.

COACHING IS ESSENTIAL BECAUSE OBEDIENCE IS EXPECTED

Make no mistake, we are all called to live in obedience to who we are and what God has called us to. The gospel propels us into a new identity where our work doesn't save us or make us acceptable. In the gospel, we are free to obey our one true Savior-King. The message of Jesus reshapes our entire life: our inner life, our schedules, our hobbies, and our vocations. The gospel changes everything and calls us into his grace in every situation; from the mundane to the spectacular. The gospel saves us into a life of joy that results in obedience. This is clear throughout Scripture:

> Teaching them to obey everything I have commanded. – Matthew 28:20

> Being no hearer who forgets, but a doer who acts. – James 1:22-25

> For we are God's workmanship, created in Christ Jesus to do good works, which God prepared in advance for us to do. – Ephesians 2:10

Coaching helps leaders understand the things God has called them to do obediently and take steps toward faithfulness. Coaching is the crucial discipleship element of a missional movement that asks: What does obedience look like? What is required to obey? How can I help you? How will you obey?

WORKING IT OUT IN YOUR CONTEXT

- What motivates your desire to be a coach or see your leaders coached?
- What outcomes do you hope to see from these coaching relationships?

CHAPTER 6 |

WHAT IS COACHING?

Original definitions of a coach:
1. A horse-drawn carriage that takes passengers from point A to point B.
2. A railroad car that takes people from point A to B.

Coaching is a relationship and a conversation that helps people get where they are headed. Missional communities want to make disciples and be used in forming communities centered around the gospel and on mission. This is a long process with many steps. However, a leader starts at point A and is looking all the way forward to point Z. The silver bullet to skip all the mess, suffering, and growth hasn't been discovered, so a coach helps leaders take one step at a time.

Missional coaching is helping leaders live what they already believe. Coaches do this by listening, offering gospel truth, resourcing, and challenging leaders to move forward into what God is calling them to do by asking simple questions. Coaches help leaders grow in clarity, perspective, and awareness. Before we get into the functions and skills of coaching, it is helpful to clarify what coaching isn't.

COACHING ISN'T SHEPHERDING
Shepherding is focused on helping the heart believe the gospel. Usually, shepherding helps disciples understand their own motivations, attitudes, and sin. Shepherding is then the process of helping people repent, believe, and find healing in Christ alone. Shepherding and gifted shepherds are needed in a

decentralized movement, too. However, missional coaching is focused on helping the disciple take steps of obedience.

Good coaching cannot exist without good shepherding, however. Without shepherding, coaching is an aid for growing legalism. Without coaching, shepherding exists in a vacuum separated from life.

COACHING ISN'T TEACHING

Teaching is focused on helping the head learn and be renewed by the truth of the gospel. Teaching helps leaders know the truth and apply it in their lives. Teaching usually involves telling, explaining, expounding, and clarifying the Bible and the message of the Bible—the gospel.

Again, good coaching cannot exist without good teaching. Without teaching, coaching helps people become busy without being grounded in discovery and depth. We become doers without understanding the "why," "what," or mystery of gospel growth. However, many Christians and leaders find themselves learning information apart from the experience of doing.

Most churches are built around well-trained shepherds and teachers. In fact, the title "pastor" is often applied to someone who is good at counseling and preaching. However, Jesus equipped his disciples to not only help people understand the gospel and believe it but to connect that knowledge and belief to daily obedience. Pastors teach, shepherd, and help disciples obey the teachings of Jesus.

COACHING ISN'T CONSULTING

Consultants are those who come in, assess the problem from the outside, and give leaders a report on what is wrong and how to fix it. Consultants tell you how to solve problems and what your next steps are. Essentially, consultants are the experts brought in to clean up the mess. I've observed many pastors within the missional movement default to this approach and call it coaching. This approach doesn't develop leaders, it isn't reproducible, and it isn't relational. Instead, it creates dependence on the consultant and leaves leaders to attempt strategies with their own missional community that worked for someone else. The leader doesn't learn how to lead by following the Spirit. Instead, the leader learns how to follow the instructions of the consultant.

Consulting missional communities doesn't work because the "consultant" isn't the expert on the missional community; its leader is. The leaders are those called, leading, and caring for their community every day. Coaches exist to help them discover their next steps. However, there are situations for telling leaders what has worked in the past, what hasn't worked, and ideas on next steps. Especially when leaders are starting out. Coaches are not experts on each missional community, but they are experts on the foundations and essentials of missional community.

COACHING ISN'T A ONE-STOP-SHOP
Coaches are dependent on discipleship-work in the domain of the head and heart. We can't coach leaders if they aren't growing in their understanding of the gospel. And we can't coach leaders if they aren't being shepherded towards repentance and faith. We don't assume leaders are in a constant place of health and learning, or that they have reached a level of nirvana or total sanctification. Shepherding must be ongoing and part of how a church cares for leaders. Likewise, teaching and learning must be ongoing, too.

Coaching is not equivalent to discipleship. Discipleship requires a community with a variety of gifts and perspectives. Coaching is simply one element in a leaders' ongoing discipleship. You may be tasked with wearing multiple hats in your church and among missional communities. If that is true, regularly ask: "Is this a coaching, shepherding, or teaching situation? God, what are you calling me to do in this moment?" Working it Out In Your Context
- How does this differ from your expectation of coaching?
- How would you clarify coaching to your leaders? What would be your definition?
- How would you separate your functions as a shepherd and teacher, from coach?

CHAPTER 7 |

THE COACHING MINDSET

A coaching structure for ongoing leadership development and encouragement is one of the substantial structural differences between a church that is made up of missional communities and a church that calls their community groups "missional communities." However, most churches, as we discussed in the last post, are full of staff who are used to telling, teaching, setting agendas, and creating strategies for their leaders. As pastors, we are more comfortable doing counseling and consulting. We're most comfortable talking about our knowledge, plans, and agendas.

A coach, however, comes into a leader's life to help him discover his agenda, and their next steps. Coaches engage leaders as a resource and as a partner who asks powerful questions (which are usually simple: What is God calling you to do? What has he made you to do in this moment? What does God call all of his people to do?). A coach equips leaders through questions, encouragement, and partnership—not telling, teaching, and consulting. How do we make the mental shift from teller to listener?

Initially, I thought this shift was simple: Ask questions. Yet, I started by asking *and* answering the questions. It was too painful to watch leaders ponder questions I could answer for them. It was too frustrating to see them come up with different plans than I had for them. I started asking leading questions that robbed them of the privilege of following God. I told them: "You can trust me. I'll tell you how to follow God." They weren't growing, and I wasn't helping. It isn't enough for us to ask questions. We have to change the mindset and assumptions about our leaders and about ourselves.

LEARN TO TRUST THEM TO LEAD

A coach has to trust the leader. The missional community leader is the expert on the people in their community, their discipleship, and their shared mission. They are called to lead and see their community learn the gospel through repentance and faith. They are committed to following Jesus in his mission. The leader is leveraging their life in significant ways to create a discipleship environment. They might not know what they are doing or what they ought to do next, but they know their people. If that is true, they can be trusted to lead. If that isn't true, they aren't leaders.

The coach does not have to be the expert on what a leader should say or do to disciple the people in her community. A coach is someone who can offer insight, stories, and resources. I'm repeatedly amazed by the ideas and next steps that leaders come up with. I'm even more amazed by the ones that "work." Here are just a few of the ideas I could have never thought of but have worked exceptionally well—so well, that missional communities throughout our city and nation copy them.

- Have a monthly planning meeting for all the rhythms and activities of the community, then break and go for it.
- Write thank you notes to Department of Human Services workers who care for foster kids and families.
- Have "Happy Hour" one night a month in the neighborhood where people gather after work to hang out and have a drink.
- Take flowers to a retirement home and begin listening to their stories and praying for them.
- Go to the rodeo as a community!
- Create a strategy board game for the older kids in the community that they play with dads as a tool to include and disciple the youth.

- Create a shared calendar everyone can post events, work schedules, vacations, etc. to keep the community on the same page.
- Have a rotation through the month of "nights out" and "nights in," so the community can grow together but also grow outwardly.
- Get together at 6am for prayer every morning for a season.

REMEMBER GOD MADE THEM

The people you're coaching are unique creations of God. Their DNA, past experiences, talents, gifts, perspectives, personalities, hobbies, interests, and their stories of faith are covered in God's grace and creativity. They are not an accident. That they are different than you should not be a surprise. The way they lead, what they lead towards, and how they move there will be unique. We are all called to make disciples, teaching them to love God and love their neighbors. How a person fulfills that calling will line up with who God made them to be. They are made in the image of God and their lives have been resurrected by Christ. Don't make them conform into your way of leading, doing things, and implementing the essentials of gospel, community, and mission. The coaching mindset says: "They are uniquely fashioned by God, and I'm excited to see what he has called them to do and be."

REMEMBER OUR IDENTITY

Jane Creswell, a renowned coach writes, "Clarity in life [is] knowing who you are and what you are called to do." As you engage in helping others move toward their calling and role in making disciples, you cannot forget who you are and who the leader is. We are all heirs, having received every spiritual blessing in Christ and through Christ we have been adopted! This means you and the person you are coaching find satisfying approval in Christ. While this is a widely accepted theological truth, it is often shelved in "strategy" or coaching sessions. We are welcomed into God's presence and family by his mercy and grace. We are loved, accepted, forgiven, and belong.

We must also remember we are made alive and empowered by the Holy Spirit. We exist in this world as witnesses of what Jesus has done for us and for the world. We are marked and sealed as God's ambassadors at work, in our homes, and in our communities. This is our identity. We are missionaries because of the work of redemption Christ has already done in us!

You also sit down for coaching conversations as citizens of the Kingdom of God. The most basic confession of a Christian ought to ring true of every session: Jesus is Lord. Both the coach and the leader are servants of Jesus. The coach comes as a servant following Jesus' agenda. They aren't there to be right, know all the answers, and force their own control and aspirations of others. Coaches are citizens of the Kingdom. Likewise the leader comes as a servant to Jesus—not their coach.

Missional coaching can only thrive when both parties submit to Jesus as Lord. Jesus is in charge of the world, the mission, and his church. Remember that you are not the king; Jesus is. You cannot be a good coach and simultaneously believe you ought to run the universe and other people's lives.

KNOW YOUR ROLE

It is also important to know what you are called to do. Coaches are equipped and released to come alongside leaders and help them move forward. Even though they may have advanced experience, they are not mentoring, not consulting, and not counseling. Coaches are servants fluent in the gospel.

Your role as a coach is to be committed to the vision of seeing gospel communities flourish on mission. You should have a working knowledge of resources and tools you can point leaders toward. However, coaches are not experts. They are simply equipped and released to come alongside leaders and help. Even though they may have advanced experience, they are not mentoring, not consulting, and not counseling. Consulting is a "telling" and problem solving roles. Coaching is a listening role that helps leaders solve problems.

As coaches, we need to remember that we are not merely here to solve problems; we are here to help leaders become more resourceful and capable in their life-long calling of making disciples. Linda Miller provides a helpful definition on Christian coaching:

Coaching is a focused Christ-centered relationship that cultivates a person's sustained growth and obedience. A coach is a person who facilitates actions that transport people from one place to another, from where they are to a new destination.

The assumption and posture of a coach is dependency. We are dependent on the Holy Spirit. Our forefront goal is to make much of Jesus and be examples of Spirit dependence. If you are to speak, speak the truth of the gospel to leaders. Remind them of who Jesus is and what he has done. Remind them of who they are.

WORKING IT OUT IN YOUR CONTEXT

- What impact do you imagine in your church or missional communities if they received help with a coaching mindset?
- On a scale of 1 to 10, how difficult is it to trust your leaders? What contributes to that trust or distrust? How can you grow in trust?
- How strongly would you agree with the statement: "Our leaders are well equipped, called, and qualified to lead"?
- Do you need to reexamine your training process to have greater confidence in your leaders?

CHAPTER 8 |

ESSENTIAL COACHING SKILLS

What skills does a coach need to be good at coaching? What makes a good coach and what do you do to become one? We've already discussed why we coach, what coaching can't do, and the mindset of a coach. Now it is time to dive into what coaching looks like. What is required to help coaches do and be what we are called to do and be?

A coach comes into a leaders' life to help them discover their agenda, their next steps, and their next lessons to teach others. Coaches engage leaders as a resource, and partner who asks powerful questions. A coach equips leaders through questions, encouragement, and partnership—not telling, teaching, and consulting.

1. ASKING POWERFUL QUESTIONS

A powerful question is one that requires the leader to think, pray, or both. This is good because as they do this leaders have to drown out the noise of the urgent and discover what is important, true, and obedient. Powerful questions help leaders gain information, insight, discovery, generate options, uncover obstacles, determine next steps. You know you have asked a good question if they can't immediately respond. Usually leaders will say, "hmm . . . that's a good question." And then they sit in silence. This is the most awkward part of being a coach. This is also the most fruitful part of coaching. For perhaps the first time in weeks and months, they are considering what is important.

Powerful Questions Are Usually Simple

- What is God calling you to do?
- What has God made and prepared you to do in this moment?
- What does God call all of his people to do?
- What is God not calling you to?
- What is hindering you from doing what you are called to do?
- What could obedience look like?
- It's okay to ask weak questions to get to powerful questions. If a leader doesn't have to think about their answer and they can quickly deliver a response, you aren't there yet.

Tips for Asking Powerful Questions

- Ask the first question in your head and formulate the question when they are done talking. In other words, listen to what they are saying. When they are done talking come up with the next question. Don't create a list of questions to spit out.
- Don't stack questions. Ask one question at a time and wait for their answer.
- Ask open-ended questions. Good questions start with what, who, how, and when. Conversely, bad questions start with: why, do, is, tell me, have, or should. These are bad because they are leading questions. We usually ask these questions when we want to say something but instead form it into a question. With closed questions, the coach is doing all the work. With open-ended questions, the leader is doing all the work.
- Pick up on things they have said and use their language, ask them to define terms they use freely—even if they seem basic. What does discipleship mean to you? What do you mean by "healthy community"? You say you want to help people to grow in their love for the word, what does "loving the word" look like? How will you know someone loves the word? These questions help

leaders clarify their own heart, intentions, and understanding. This is crucial equipping. Don't do it for them!

- Ask question with plural options. For example, "What are things that can be done?" "What are some ideas?"

2. OFFERING OBSERVATIONS

Another crucial skill is offering observations, themes, or patterns to a leader. As you listen to a leader, think about what is being shared, the context surrounding what is being shared, and what isn't being shared. Then, when you have the opportunity speak directly about what you are seeing, ask them to name it and explain what you see. This process forces leaders to see their own assumptions or might jar them into seeing their problem or opportunity in a new light. Mostly, it helps them see themselves.

I was once coaching a leader through the process of discovering their calling, and for them that meant church planting. They were struggling with their calling and where they would be. He had tried different avenues and aspects of ministry. He had experience as a youth minister, international church planter, and worship leader. One day we sat down for a coaching meeting, and he described that he was learning about caring for children who lost parents through accidents, death, separation, addiction, etc. Never before had he done this, but on that day, he wept.

As he was wiping his tears away, I asked, "We've been talking about church planting, where, how, and what you are called to do for a long time. We've even talked about the people in your community you are discipling and you have discipled. This is the first time you've ever shed a tear. What do you think that means?"

This conversation blossomed into a wonderful experience of discovering how his entrepreneurial gifts, love for the church, and love for orphans work together to form a beautiful calling. He became part of a team that led our church into holistic-relational care for children in foster care and foster families. He also realized the business he started employs mostly young men who did not have active fathers in their lives. It started with observing his tears and asking him what he thought it meant.

3. SPEAKING ENCOURAGEMENT

The world is in an encouragement drought. We are able to track approval—through likes, retweets, and comments like: "You're Beautiful Girl!" Tragically, this isn't encouragement of a human and the way they are following Jesus. This is cheap affirmation and its help is fleeting in the life of a person. Leaders need to be reminded they're on the right track, they're moving forward, and God is at work. More importantly, we all need to be shown the transformation God is doing as we follow Jesus.

Encouragement, as a coaching skill is not a matter of boosting the esteem of our leaders. Rather, it is crucial to our worship of God and his glorious works. Encouragement is important because it is how we notice and remember God's gracious transformation of our lives. Sam Crabtree in his book *Practicing Affirmation* makes this connection well:

> *"To affirm Christlikeness in transformed believers is to affirm what Christ purchased with his own blood. I am suggesting that we rob God of praise by not pointing out his reflection in the people he has knit together in his image."*

When a coach and leader exclusively move from one strategy, issue, concern, or opportunity to the next, they miss the transforming work God is doing through their obedience. Through coaching, we see God do miraculous things like give confidence to the cowardly, patience to the uptight, grace to the perfectionist, and hope to the despairing. If we see inattentive and disobedient leaders turn their ear to God in prayer and then take steps of faith, we ought to celebrate! This is what encouragement is in missional coaching: bringing clarity to the work that God is doing in and through the life of the leader and celebrating it!

Tips on Good Encouragement

Encouragement ought to be specific. Meaning you acknowledge and celebrate a real action, attitude, repentance, and character growth in the leader. Good encouragement isn't a generic: "You've grown, and you're doing a good job." Instead it is: "You've grown as a leader, establishing boundaries and understanding your limits. Just look at last week when you told a person in your community that you couldn't help them but needed to take a day to rest after a week of travel! That's huge!"

Encouragement ought to be genuine. You can't do encouragement well if you are doing it simply because you think you ought to do it. Instead, you truly have to be caught up in the wonder, grace, and transformation the person is on. You must agree with the encouragement and not force it.

Encouragement ought to be timely. Try to encourage your leaders soon after they have experienced and done the thing you are encouraging them in. Encouragement looses its impact when you say in June: "You guys really did a great job celebrating Christmas as a community! Wow, I don't remember the details, but I remember thinking it was good."

Encouragement ought to be relevant to the conversation. I've frequently been caught in the desire to encourage a leader so badly it comes from left field and isn't about what they are experiencing at all in the moment.

Encouragement ought to be theologically true and aligned with the gospel. For example, you wouldn't say, "Look at all the people you are saving! Wow, remember that guy who didn't have anything going for him, and then you saved him!" Unless you are coaching Jesus, this is heresy. Instead you might say, "God really has you in a fruitful season right now. He is using you to bring people into the family of God, and you are physically showing God's love to people through your sacrifice and generosity. The gospel is being clarified through that."

Encouragement doesn't have to be about them or something they are doing well. This one is huge. Many times, if not all the time, a clear and relevant articulation of the gospel and the pilgrimage that is discipleship, with its ups and downs, is encouragement. Often, this can be a reading of a passage of

Scripture that you think is helpful. Remember, you are bringing clarity to the work God has and is doing.

Follow encouragement with a question to help them gain clarity or get unstuck. Questions after an exhortation can be powerful. For example, you could ask:

- What do you think is causing that growth?
- What has changed that allows you to be believing and doing these things?
- How do you see your growth in this area?
- What would help you excel even more in this transformation?

4. DELIVERING CLEAR AND CONCISE MESSAGES

Sometimes coaches get to preach and teach. They get to provide punchy messages to help leaders move forward. These are short! Think typically of seven words or less. Think in terms of bullet point messages, not three part sermons.

What kind of clear and concise messages are helpful?

- Short story from a coach's life about a similar situation.
- Parables and illustrations from life.
- A quote from a book, a passage of Scripture, or a recent sermon.
- Useful information on how the church is organized or principles on discipleship.
- A short training on discipleship, spiritual disciplines, missional community life, etc.

The aim of these short messages is to bring clarity and instruction. Direct messages can also offer a leader a new way to think about their issue, opportunity, or calling. These should be used sparingly: one direct message per coaching conversation.

Once, I was coaching a leader who was struggling with being a doer and not resting. He was filled with anxieties about money, work, home improvements, leading, and comparing his work to others. He has a cocktail of idols that completely stop him from resting—even though he has stated that's what he wants to grow in and lead his community in. I said, "You have a lot things you are thinking about, do you pray about them?" He said he didn't.,I followed up with this direct message, "We don't pray about things we think are in our control, our problem, or our mess." He nodded and as that sank in I shared a story of how I learned to pray and yield control to God. I asked him, "What would it look like if you yielded control by praying for just five minutes?" This unlocked a new pattern and next step beyond simply telling himself to just rest over and over again.

5. RESOURCING

Though we can occasionally put on our "trainer" hat, a key aspect of this coaching relationship is understanding the leaders' learning style and being able to point them to resources and tools that will help them learn. As coaches we often drawing upon our experiences, resources, and tools to help leaders move forward. This one is simple and hard at the same time. It is simple because we just share resources with people. It is hard because we tend to think that what was good for us is good for everyone else.

For example, one of my preferred ways to learn is through books—thick and dense books. I get to coach many leaders who also love to read and wrestle through long books. Many others don't want to read and if they do, they want it to be short and accessible. I don't like podcasts or training videos, but many I coach do. One of the selfless acts of a coach is to be knowledgeable about resources that could help those you are coaching.

One of the best ways to learn what tools and resources to offer is to ask, "What sort of things would help you in this next step? What kind of resources do you like?"

6. RELYING ON THE HOLY SPIRIT THROUGH PRAYER

The final and most important skill of a coach is prayer. As a coach you will learn to pray before, during, and after conversations with leaders. You pray for God to make it clear what to ask, what to say, what to give them. You depend on God to make the conversation everything he wants it to be. Ask God to lead the leader. Ask God to lead you.

COACHING IS THE ART OF BEING A GOOD FRIEND

Coaching is an art because it's a relationship, and it's a conversation. Both require a level of self-understanding and interest in others. The skills described in this chapter are foundational, not just to coaching but to being human and living in community. These skills are powerful because we so rarely listen, encourage, pray, or speak concise challenging messages to one another. At first these skills seem awkward. However, as you apply them in life, you realize they are simply the way to make and be a good friend. As you step into intentionally coaching leaders, begin by experimenting with these skills in your relationships, with your children, spouse, roommates, and neighbors. Notice their reaction and your reaction.

WORKING IT OUT IN YOUR CONTEXT

- Which coaching skill do you think your church is particularly strong in? Which skill do you see weakness?
- In your strength, how can that be used to greater fruit?
- In your weakness, how can you grow in that skill in everyday life (outside of coaching)?
- Are there other skills you think are required in your context to coach leaders well?

CHAPTER 9 |

THE COACHING CONVERSATIONS

INTENTIONAL MOMENTS WITH LEADERS

Over the last several chapters we've unpacked what coaching is and is not, how to be a coach, and the skills required. Now we turn our attention to the coaching conversations themselves. What do you actually do when you sit down with a leader? How does coaching happen? I've learned it requires preparation and a plan or pattern of questions to guide the conversation. The goal is to have intentional conversations that foster both belief and obedience. Conversations like that don't happen by accident.

BEFORE YOU EVEN SIT DOWN: PRE-WORK

Pre-work for the Coach

Spend time reviewing your past notes with this leader, praying, and getting into the coaching mindset. Refresh yourself on the required skills in coaching. Most importantly, pray for the leader, their family, and their missional community. Ask God to reveal what is important. Look for patterns or issues in your notes that might need to be discussed.

Pre-work for the Leader

The leader has to come ready, too. They have to come ready to "work" and process with the coach. To do that, they need to put some thought into their time, too. Here are three broad sets of questions to help leaders prepare to be coached.

Where am I in life?
What is going on? What is God teaching me? What is your community teaching me?

Where is my community?
Where are we as people? What has God done through us? What are we wrestling with? Where do we have unity/disunity?

Where is my community headed?
Where is it that God is leading us? What does "thy kingdom come" in my community feel like? What are we called to? How is God stretching us? What season are we in as a community?

WHEN YOU SIT DOWN: THE COACHING CONVERSATION

Below, I want to provide a model for guiding a conversation that works from long-term thinking to small next-steps. This is the pattern I follow. I will lay out the major topics or shifts in conversations as well as my my go-to questions and follow-up questions to clarify if a leader gets stuck. While I've never had a conversation that perfectly followed this path, this roadmap is very helpful! You may find that this conversation model doesn't work for you. Don't worry; there are others models in the appendix.

Sprinkled through each of these big categories or questions are times where you would ask follow-up questions, offer observations, and give direct messages.

Connect and Pray

Pretty self-explanatory. Talk about each others' kids, weekends, marriages, etc. Pray for one another as peers in the pilgrimage of discipleship.

Big Picture

Where are we headed in the long-term? What is your community becoming? These questions help the leader get their

74

head out of the weeds or their weekly crisis and think about the big picture. This alone is a blessing to leaders!

Small Picture

What do we need to talk about today? Thinking about this coaching meeting, where do you want to be at the end of this? What do you want us to accomplish today? What could we talk about? The time spent in coaching conversation is about discovering what is important in the short-term: the one thing.

Narrowing the Conversation

What is next? What obstacles do you face? What are some of the most pressing roadblocks your community is facing in moving where you feel God is leading? What opportunities do you have? This series of questions really brings the leader into processing what obedience to their calling looks like.

Gaining Clarity and Counting the Cost

What can be done about it? What is in your control? What is the cost? What are you willing to pay? Are these permanent obstacles, barriers, issues? These questions really help to unearth the commitment or desire a leader has to take a next step. It also helps them realize some issues are beyond their control.

Brainstorming

What are some potential next steps? What can be done? This is a great time to brainstorm and come up with ideas together.

Committing to Obedience

What will you do about it? When will you do it? These questions are about accountability. Even if their next step is to pray, ask, "When will you pray? How will you pray? Who could pray with you?" The goal is to make it concrete for their sake. If the next step is to wait and rest because it is out of their control ask,

"How will you avoid trying to take control again? What has to happen to allow you to do that? What does resting look like?"

Resourcing

How can I help? This is when we get to offer our service and help out! Many times this is answer is, "Keep asking me about this."

Pray and Part Ways

As you leave, pray for the commitments and next steps that have been planned. Also, part ways with clarity. I usually reflect back to the leader what they have decided to do, and what I am going to do. This parting of ways is important. The leader is usually rushing off to work or home after this conversation. A summary of what was talked about and what they are going to do is helpful. It is also a helpful moment for the coach to realize the leader is now re-engaging the world they inhabit.

FOLLOWING A COACHING CONVERSATION

Take notes about what was discussed, what the next step(s) were, and anything they said that you want to add to your prayers for them. Pray for their community. Personally, I have to spend some time in prayer to give up trying to control the leader and community after I meet with them. I want to do the next steps and I want to lead that community my way, and I get stressed trying to control it from a distance after the coaching session. I've learned to pray afterwards as a discipline for my own good.

WORKING IT OUT IN YOUR CONTEXT
- As you look at this model, which moment in the conversation is most exciting for you? What is the most daunting?
- How will you ask leaders to prepare and how will you follow-up your coaching meetings?

CHAPTER 10 |

STARTING COACHING RELATIONSHIPS

HOW TO BEGIN WELL

Starting is an exciting part of a leader's journey and coaching ministry. You are stepping into a relationship that you hope reminds the leader of the gospel, nurtures their role within a community, and helps that leader move forward in obedience to their calling.

The first meetings are important for momentum in the relationship. You have to work together to help develop the leader's calling, vision, hopes, and dreams for their community. It is only with this initial discovery that you can coach and build. A leaders' vision sets the agenda for forward movement. Throughout the coaching relationship you will hold their vision and mission for them, fight for it, remind them of it, and celebrate it being realized.

INVITE LEADERS INTO THIS RELATIONSHIP

Help the leader understand what they are getting themselves into. Allow them to ask questions and cast vision for how you want to help them. This is crucial because, as a coach, you are setting the table for a deep relationship.

A coach begins the relationship in discovery mode and reinforcing what this relationship will be like. Often, community leaders will think their "coach" is a supervisor that will check in on how they are doing like quality control. You are, in fact, there to come alongside them as they lead. You are coming to help them remember the gospel and calling. You are there to help them fight for faith and obedience.

The leader also needs to know coaching requires something of them, too. They aren't there to give a report and receive their marching orders. A leader must come to coaching meetings ready to work, share, and explore what God is calling them to do. Coaching is a relationship designed to help them hear God's voice and obey him.

THE FIRST FOUR MEETINGS OF A COACHING RELATIONSHIP

- Get to know each other and share stories.
- Help discover and clarify their vision for their community of saints.
- Help discover and clarify their community's role in God's mission.
- Begin to grow in awareness of their role as a leader of that community on mission.

MEETING #1: KNOW EACH OTHER AND YOUR STORIES

Begin your first meeting by sharing your life stories. This is the best way to start this relationship as brothers or sisters in Christ. Avoid jumping straight into troubleshooting, strategies, or dreaming. Our experiences, lessons learned through education, and God's work in our lives are woven together to form whole people. Skipping this step robs you of celebrating God's work in the past and as you move forward together. It also puts Christ's work at the center of your coaching relationship. Lastly, it helps you coach and the leader be coached because you have an awareness for where each of you are as deep individuals in God's story. Our friends at Soma created a guide that helps folks share their story well and concisely. We use it often. However, the main points you're hoping to each hit on as you take turns sharing are:

- Where did you come from? (Family of origin, home environment, etc.)
- How did Christ intersect your story?

78

- How have you experienced community?
- Where are you today?
- Where do you imagine your future going?

Unique to this particular coaching relationship you may want to ask about their hopes for community in general, friends who don't know Jesus, and the poor. Likewise, ask questions about their past leadership experiences, things they want to avoid, lessons learned, etc.

You will likely discover that many leaders are not aware of their own strengths and weaknesses as leaders. They also are not aware of their personal perspective on the world and how that impacts their decisions and leadership. They probably don't even consciously think about their gifts, values, or personality unless they come from a corporate or organizational environment that fosters self-discovery.

MEETING #2: KNOW THEIR COMMUNITY AND VISION

Gain understanding of the vision, missional focus, and history of the leader's community. Your goal in this conversation is to create space for the leader to dream and come to clarity about what he is pursuing. Ask them to imagine their community thriving in the gospel and their identity in Christ.

Ask them questions like these:

- Who is in your community? What is easy to love about them? What's hard to love about them?
- What do you hope to see God do in them?
- What does health look like for your community?
- What would it look like for your community to be a family?
- What doors would have to be opened?
- What reconciliation is required?
- What faith in the gospel would be required?
- Where is easiest for you to pray for the gospel to break in? In other words, what do you find yourself hoping will happen in this group of people?

Lastly, you will want to end this conversation by brining it to a focus on the future and on a few ideas and prayers for this community:

- What are some goals that would lend itself to seeing your community become a family of servants for this year?
- What one thing could your community work towards together?
- What could this coaching relationship focus on over the next several months?

MEETING #3: KNOW THEIR MISSION AND ROLE IN THE MISSION

Next, you want to hear about where God has called this particular community to show the gospel and proclaim the gospel. The goal of this conversation is to help the leader articulate their mission or grow in knowing how they will decide their mission. Where has God placed them in the city? What are the barriers to the gospel in their neighborhood? Who has God placed in their lives? How has God called them to care for the poor and marginalized?

Many new communities have no idea where to start and many leaders have a long list of ideas and potential. It is helpful to simply put those on the table in this conversation and to pray together for wisdom and clarity on this community's calling. You don't have to force it. If they do not know what their shared mission is, it is better to ask questions along these lines:

- How could your community discover their shared mission?
- What are the steps, timeline, and principles that will help your community know what their shared mission is?
- How will the community pray together and what will help that season of prayer?
- What are some barriers to discovering it?

80

- How will you know your community has unity and clarity?

MEETING #4: WORK TOGETHER TO DISCOVER THEIR LEADERSHIP CALLING

Perhaps the most important early coaching relationship conversation is about leadership. The only way for coaching to work is for the leader to know and understand their leadership calling. A leader must understand what it means for them to be a leader. Leaders need to know how God designed them to lead, how God gifted them to lead, and, by default, how God hasn't called them to lead. However, this conversation is about more than simply how or why a leader leads. It is fundamental for the coaching relationship to begin with base level understanding of what is and is not the responsibility of a leader. A few helpful questions in growing in this understanding for the leader might be:

- What is your particular role in the process of your community becoming what you hope it will become?
- What isn't your role in the process?
- What will you definitely delegate?
- What will you definitely *not* delegate?

Go over any questions they might have about the leaders' role description and ask questions about how they plan and envision cultivating a community of gospel growth and practice.

TIP: FIGURE OUT THE LOGISTICS BEFORE YOU START

This is a short list of logistics to consider with coaching, and it doesn't take much. If you don't nail it down in the beginning, logistics can be an energy drain that keeps the coaching relationship from thriving:

- Decide on a method of communication: e-mail, text, phone calls, etc.
- Decide a regular time, place, and frequency for coaching?

- If you are wearing multiple hats (elder, staff-member, friend, etc) you want to be clear when you are having a coaching meeting and when you are doing other things like shepherding, counseling, training, and hanging-out. These clear distinctions will prove helpful in your relationships.

TIP: USE THEIR OWN LANGUAGE

As you begin to hear their vision for gospel community and mission and engage in discussions with them, use their own words and language. You are helping them clarify and own their calling as a leader of a community of disciples. One of the best ways to hijack that progress is to ignore the words they have for it. For example, if a leader is describing his hope that the kingdom of God will break into their lives and neighborhood, don't refer to their hope as God pouring his Spirit out or the gospel advancing. They are using this language because it makes sense to them. You can challenge their language and help them clarify their own hope by asking:

- What do you mean by the kingdom breaking in?
- What would that look like?
- How would someone who doesn't believe experience that?

WORKING IT OUT IN YOUR CONTEXT

- How have you established your relationship with leaders in the past? How much clarity, purpose, or depth did those relationships have?
- What would it look like for you and your team to begin relationships this way?
- Do you have an intentional progression in your coaching relationships? How do you build trust and understanding? How do you facilitate movement forward?

CHAPTER 11 |

STAGES OF A COACHING RELATIONSHIP

I believe in coaching missional community leaders because it makes them better leaders. Not just today but in the future. Coaching helps leaders in their present circumstances think through the discipleship environment and the shepherding of their community in the gospel and mission. Coaching helps leaders move forward today. The big fruit from coaching, however, comes from the process of coaching. Through coaching and experience, leaders grow from enthusiastic, yet fearful, to gospel motivated and confident. Here are the four phases of the coaching relationship. Notice the shifts in the leaders and the coaching approach.[1]

PHASE 1: LEADERS LEARN WHAT IS IMPORTANT
In this phase, the leader really wants to lead and is super excited about doing it. They are motivated by the gospel and called to lead an MC. They just have no real idea how to do it. They've been trained, and they've seen someone do it.

The initial phase of a coaching relationship focused on leading a missional community is coach driven. The new leader has lots of enthusiasm and passion to see disciples made within a community centered on the gospel and on mission. They have been trained, and they have participated in a missional community. They know the what and why, just haven't learned

---

1These phases are based on Ken Blanchard's "Situational Leadership Development". I'm completely indebted to this philosophy I've applied to missional community leadership.

the how. Imagine how someone starts a new job, or freshman in college, or athlete on a team. They are excited to be there, but they really don't know what to do.

Furthermore, they don't even know what is important and what is a priority. They have high enthusiasm but low competency and confidence. A coach's job here is to teach the leader how to filter through what is important and how to gauge their current season within the context of long-haul discipleship.

Coaching Approach in Phase 1: Here's Some Plans, Which One Would You Like to Do?

In this phase, the leader is most served by directive coaching: clearly articulated direction or clear choices for next steps. The leader doesn't know, so the coach gets to provide that for them. In this phase of MC leadership, the coach meetings should be set by the coach: Let's talk about communication, logistics, common mission, and gospel foundation. Also, the leader is hungry to be given training wheels: "Here's a simple curriculum to follow to lay a foundation." So a coach might give them choices, discuss each, and let the leader chose (but even the choice is more about them picking their preferred training wheels). However, in this stage, the leader is learning to think about their leadership and their skills.

PHASE 2: LEARNING TO PROCESS WELL

This is the most difficult phase and when most consider quitting. They still don't know much about leadership, and they aren't motivated anymore. There's difficulty, hardships, and overall pain from serving people. Again picture the new job, new school, new team dynamic. The honeymoon is over, but you're still new and the learning curve is still happening!

Leaders aren't burned out, yet. They are learning they can't change people. They now have experienced this truth first hand. They now know that people, no matter how well loved, do not respond the way we want them to. Leaders need lots of support and lots of direction.

In phase one, the leader has high enthusiasm and low competence. In phase two, the leader has low enthusiasm and low competence. They don't know what they are doing and aren't that excited about it anymore!

Coaching Approach in Phase 2: Let's Make a Plan Together

This phase is marked by giving leaders freedom to create the next steps alongside their coach. They must be pushed to realize they know more than they think! This is a crucial point in their leadership development where they might prefer to avoid their community. However, the coaching process forces them to process and pray about it regularly. As they process with a coach, they get better at it. They grow in their ability to articulate their concerns, hopes, and ideas.

This is when we introduce the concept of Seasonal Focus. This is a singular spiritual and transformative goal for a group. It likely comes from their missional commitment or a discipline that can be engaged communally. The coaching questions are: What one thing would be good for your community to focus on? followed by "How will you focus on that? What types of learning, experiences, shared times, would be required?" In this phase, the coach is giving the leader the frame-work for a seasonal focus as well as giving input into the leader's plan they are making.

Also, during this phase, it is important for the coach to demonstrate prayer for the community—spending lots of time simply praying for the community together is HUGE! I struggle to do that, but this is when we as the coaches have the crucial opportunity to show that God moves not our strategies.

PHASE 3: LEADERS LEARN TO LISTEN TO THEMSELVES

This phase is where typical "missional coaching" takes place. This is the time where leaders feel like they know what they are doing, how to care for people, and how they lead. More than anything they need someone who can help them process what they already know and get support. They need to know they aren't alone! They need lots of support and encouragement but not lots of direction

Coaching Approach in Phase 3: How Can I Help You Make a Plan?

This is phase is the longest lasting and just great. This is where leaders come ready to work on specific issues with the coach and expect the coach to help them come up with a next step instead of looking to the coach to give them the next step. However, these leaders might struggle with communal awareness. This is why resources like "Picture of Health" can come in handy.

PHASE 4: LEADERS LEARN TO INFLUENCE OTHERS

This is when you've got an expert leader. They don't need to give you reports or updates. They have learned how to process what is going on and how to follow the Spirit's leading. They may call you occasionally to talk through specific situations and turn to you as the pastor, but not so much as the coach. Coaching meetings begin to look like prayer and friendship times. The leaders are mostly looking for relationship and connection.

Coaching Approach in Phase 4: How Can I Help You With Your Plan? How Can I Support You?

The coach is now asking how they can resource the plans already created by the leader. In this phase the coach wants to spend time hearing about what God is doing and teaching the leader. This is the moment you get to be the cheerleader. At this point, the coaching meetings take on a deeply spiritual and focused connection to what God has done and is doing. You can look back and see how the leader has grown in confidence and their ability to listen to God and walk in faithfulness as leaders.

They have walked through trails, conflicts, and victories. They now know how to process them and how to ask for help.

WORKING IT OUT IN YOUR CONTEXT

- What phase of leadership do you gravitate towards as a coach?
- What stage do you think each of your leaders are currently in and what approach should you use with them to further their growth?
- Is there a trend within your context? How can you improve as a "situational" coach?

CHAPTER 12 |

MULTIPLYING COACHES

Remember, coaching is essential for a sustained missional community movement. If you are committed to decentralized discipleship, you must make ongoing investments in leaders. If this is true and if every leader needs to be coached, you will need to multiply coaches. You probably can't coach all the leaders in your care, and even if you can today, you won't be able to in a year or two when they have all multiplied. Therefore, we have to not only become proficient coaches ourselves but identify, train, and release new coaches into this role. This is the next level of investing in leaders: multiplying coaches and developing a structure for that to happen. This requires some aspect of knowing what you are looking for in coaches and creating a process for people to start coaching with excellence.

IDENTIFYING VOLUNTEER COACHES
This first step in implementing movement-wide coaching is identifying people who would make good coaches. I've often been asked what makes a good coach and what is their profile? Is there a personality type? The truth is I've seen excellent extrovert and introvert coaches. I've also seen some fantastic artistic free spirits as coaches and wonderful systematic engineer coaches. I've found it is best to look for particular strengths when looking for coaches regardless of perspective and personality. Here are the top three strengths I'm looking for in addition to the raw coaching skill discussed in chapter nine.

1. Maximizer

This person loves to get the most out of everything. They want to take things—but mostly people—and help them experience their full potential. A maximizer will continually nudge someone forward and help them press on. This is a crucial quality in a coach. Symptoms of maximizers: They can make $5 for lunch go a long way, they are always finding ways of developing themselves, and they get excited about anyone who is trying something new and taking forward steps in their calling.

How do you know someone isn't a maximizer? If they enjoy tearing other people down. If they see flaws when others see opportunities. If they focus on what is missing more than they focus on what is present.

2. Catalyst

A catalyst is someone who ignites situations. They like to dream with people and get things going. They hear a new idea and immediately begin brainstorming how far that idea could go and imagine what the first few steps might be. Overall, their excitement and encouragement throws fuel on the fire of an idea or calling.

3. Process Oriented

This is another way of saying patient. A good coach has the ability to know there is a long way to go from where someone is today and where they want to be. A coach can see the distance and not crumble under it or attempt to speed it along. Instead, a good coach is someone who enjoys the journey as much as the arrival.

A VOLUNTEER COACH'S ROLE DESCRIPTION

After you have identified potential coaches you have to ask them to step into a defined role with defined expectations. Below is what I share with potential coaches who are processing this role and contribution in our church.

A Missional Community Coach will likely have experience leading a missional community and be committed to the vision of seeing missional communities flourish in the gospel and shared mission. They will have a working knowledge of the resources and tools accessible to leaders. They are not better than anyone else or the boss of missional communities; they are equipped and released to come alongside leaders and help them move forward. Even though they may have advanced experience, they are not mentoring, not consulting and not counseling. Coaches are not experts but servants who are fluent in the gospel. At Bread&Wine, we ask coaches for a one-year commitment with opportunities to reassess each year.

Here are the regular expectations we have for volunteer coaches within Bread&Wine to help you develop your own:

- Meet with leaders you are coaching once or twice a month, depending on the experience and needs of the leader(s).
- Help leaders write their own Leadership Development Plan once a year. Use it as a template for your coaching conversations.
- Pray for leaders you are coaching and their communities. It is usually helpful to track specific prayer requests in a journal or smartphone. Also, many leaders have found it helpful to set up reminders in the calendars for this.
- Keep track of your coaching conversations using a basic spreadsheet. This takes about ten minutes following a coaching conversation and will help you and other coaches track where these conversations are going.
- Participate in ongoing coaching trainings, Missional Community leader meetings, and an annual leaders's retreat.

EQUIPPING AND RELEASING PROCESS

Once you've identified and invited potential coaches, you will need to equip and release them into the role of coaching. Below is the general outline for equipping and releasing coaches within Bread&Wine. Some coaches will come to this role with more experience and confidence, others less. Therefore, this isn't a hard and fast "curriculum" but rather a general outline bathed in experience and best practices.

How do you start coaching?
- Attend the basic Coaching Training.
- Read Coaching 101 by Bob Logan and Multiply Together
- Sit down with an experienced coach to discuss what has been learned and talk through coaching tools.
- Evaluate your capacity for coaching leaders.
- Have three coaching sessions with another person who is getting equipped in coaching. Split the time between you for both being coached and coaching, and receiving and giving feedback—twenty-five minutes for coaching, five minutes for feedback, and then switch.
- Is God asking me to coach leaders during this season?
- How many leaders do I have the capacity to coach?
- What are the times that will work well for me to coach leaders?
- What type of leaders would be best for me to coach?
- After this process, you will meet with the elder who oversees coaching to discuss the leaders you will be assigned to coach.
- Start coaching! As you have questions and concerns, stay in contact with your elders.
- Attend regular leader meetings and trainings.

WORKING IT OUT IN YOUR CONTEXT
- How many coaches do you need?
- What would you require of them? What training do they need?
- How will you assign coaches to communities?

EPILOGUE

Leaders and communities need you, their pastor and coach. While we've walked through many concepts, approaches, and processes for multiplying communities in this book, the greatest asset you can provide a leader is your availability to them. Leaders need your story and your presence with them in the present. They need your spiritual, emotional, and physical availability to walk with them as they learn to love God, love their community, and love their neighbors.

We have a tendency to make things complicated; however, the task at hand is simple: make disciples through sharing the gospel. Communities that are growing in their belief in the gospel and receiving God's love multiply. Pastors who love their people and love their city see fruit in their own lives and the lives of others. Therefore, let these simple questions from Henri Nouwn, operate as a self-coaching exercise as you equip the saints for the work of the ministry:

> *Did I offer peace today? Did I bring a smile to someone's face? Did I say words of healing? Did I let go of my anger and resentment? Did I forgive? Did I love? These are the real questions. I must trust that the little bit of love that I sow now will bear many fruits, here in this world and the life to come.*

APPENDIXES: TOOLS FOR COACHES

APPENDIX I: TRAINING MISSIONAL COMMUNITY LEADERS

While everything we do in missional community life is geared at maturing and developing disciples of Jesus; we must proactively train leaders to start new missional communities that engage new neighborhoods and provide new communities for people to grow in.

Training leaders is hard work. Training costs you time, energy, and resources. Most pay the cost without a clear process and plan. In other words, we invest the time, energy, and resources in training without a thoughtful and consistent process. After all that hard work, we still come back to our whiteboards asking the questions:

- How do leaders develop, grow, and learn?
- How do I give them everything they need so they can lead effectively?
- What are the possible and reasonable outcomes to expect from training?
- How much training would be too much?
- What does every leader need to know to lead a missional community?

WHAT DO THEY *NEED* TO LEAD A MISSIONAL COMMUNITY?

We answer this question by looking at a leader's role description and work backwards. We can see leaders need multiple levels of equipping. A new missional community leader needs information or, more precisely, theology. They need to learn and interact with the theory and philosophy behind missional community life. They have to examine it biblically and hear from people who have done it before. The leaders we train essentially need a classroom environment.

A new missional community leader needs skills. They need to learn how to speak the gospel. The need to see how each piece fits together. You can't learn how without doing. The leaders we train will need time practicing and growing in skills. This doesn't simply happen by being in a missional community! Observation, feedback, and assessment is hard work that allows leaders to grow through experience.

A new missional community leader needs character growth. Their motivations, their sins, their practice of repentance and faith, and their processing of life's circumstances is perhaps the most crucial component. A leader needs time by themselves within their own mind and heart to internalize all the information, experiences, and spiritual formation that leads them to leadership.

LEARNING ENVIRONMENTS

While pursuing the technological advancement in education, David Thornburg, Walden University professor and researcher, realized there are four timeless spaces or environments where all humans learn. He argues all humans develop their understating of topics, issues, and problems within a society through four interconnected environments: the campfire, the watering hole, the cave, and life. To train anyone successfully, we must engage each environment. As you will see these are quite intuitive and if neglected, weakened.

The "Campfire": Traditional Classroom

In the campfire space is where we learn meaning—the big stories that help us find meaning and the common principles of life. The campfire was the first classroom. The first space of intentional training. Sitting in a circle, the audience listen to the wise storyteller expound on their existence far beyond entertainment. This is a crucial space. Despite all our advancement in technology and understanding of human development, one cannot escape the necessity for listening and learning directly from others. We often describe this as the "traditional classroom."

Within the traditional training we seek to teach people:

- The gospel, christian community, and shared mission
- The philosophies and approaches of missional community life
- The role and functions of leadership
- Stories of how the gospel has taken root in our lives
- The tools and next steps of community development

The strength of the traditional classroom is that it creates a common core for all leaders. If you develop a standard training all leaders go through, you will have strength in common language, common approaches, and common skills. It's also true that the classroom is limited. Within it you are provided an image, a common story, and a philosophy that has to then be tested in real life.

The "Watering Hole": Experience in a Missional Community

All humans also need the watering hole to process new ideas, philosophies, and approaches to life. While the campfire was the gathering place in the evening to hear from the wise, the watering hole was the gathering place in the day to hear from each other. Thornburg describes this space as social learning among peers, or dialogue. As we train people in the traditional classroom, we have to send them out to gather and grow around shared ideas. We all need time to discuss, process, and explore with peers to truly understand.

As a leader of leaders, we have to acknowledge the need to nurture gathering points for emerging leaders to discuss and grow. This, by the way, is an uncontrollable and unguided learning environment. It's the people who are training each other. They are digesting the "campfire." It is also where people share their stories, their experiences, their fears, and their ideas in the most unfiltered way.

Within the missional community approach, there isn't a better way than within a missional community. The best way for emerging leaders to grow in the concepts of missional community is to be within one. This is the best environment to grow alongside others, to ask questions, to pursue doubts, and to share ideas.

The "Cave": Making it Their Own Through Reflection

The cave, or reflective learning, is the space where people internalize for themselves and within themselves. They take ownership of ideas *and* their continued learning. The purpose is for the learned to become aware of their own life, reflecting on how all that has been taught is true. It is also the space in which decisions to change, move forward, and engage happen. This is the most challenging space for people in our culture to engage in; however, it is perhaps the most crucial. Thornburg describes the modern challenges to engage the "cave":

> *In today's hectic life, there is precious little time for quiet contemplation, yet, as Newton found, it is through such contemplation that some of the greatest discoveries are made. We should ask what the consequences are for a society that doesn't value the kind of thinking that takes place during the quiet periods of reflection . . . this is how we have become human doings instead of human beings."*

Once we pause and think, we are confronted with the things we don't understand, the things that aggravate us, and the things we are curious about. We must work to create spaces and time to reflect and internalize. This means our leadership retreats and training sessions can't be dominated by social time, activity, and content. What many of our leaders desperately need is not new content but a context to process, pray, and think. In our leadership role description, we outline the expectation that leaders will spend one hour each week praying for their community and one hour thinking about their community. By making reflection time a priority in a leaders' training, you are creating sustainable habits that will serve them when they're responsible for a community.

The challenge, however, is not simply giving people a place to reflect in but also things to reflect on. The cave is not undirected time. It is in this area that we operate as spiritual directors. Working with leaders in training to "enter the cave" and reflect on specific things. We give them assignments, questions, and exercises to work through to help leaders grow in faith, character, and spiritual formation.

Through "Life": Learning by Doing and Leading

Lastly, there is the space called life. As a seminary student I listened to lectures on biblical interpretation and preaching. I was engaged by my peers during breaks, study sessions, and in preparation for finals. Through the course, I also read and saw all my thinking spill out into assignments. However, it was in preaching to my church that all that learning began to matter. It was in real life that it became alive—that I saw my learning and where I returned to those class notes, books, and peers to remember what I had learned.

A well-rounded leadership training program will have an apprenticeship component where new leaders observe and lead under an experienced leader within the context of a missional community. In this way, it is no longer theory to be appreciated but a life to participate in. Within this environment we try to be intentional with a new leader's growth.

Here are four ways we help leaders grow by doing.

1. Honest Assessment of Gifts, Strengths, and Perspective

We have a two-hour long assessment we do with leaders where we hear their story, perspectives, and areas of strength and growth. We also utilize personality assessments to help the leader understand their gifts. This assessment process helps us know the strengths and opportunities for growth. Much of this information gets added to their Leadership Development Plan.

2. Real Responsibility

This means we give leaders in training jobs, tasks, and areas of oversight over the course of their preparation. For example, hospitality, leading a discipleship group of men or women, facilitating the discussions, or being the missional leader.

3. Constructive Feedback

As they exercise leadership, we give them feedback on how it went, how their leadership was received, and how they can improve. We also hear how the leaders are feeling, thinking, and wanting to improve.

4. Participate in Regular Leader Meetings and Discussions

Every leadership team of a missional community gets together regularly to discuss the direction, next steps, and state of their community. We invite leaders in training into these times to observe the shepherding aspect of leadership.

PUTTING IT IN YOUR CONTEXT

- What is your leadership training approach and process?
- Is your leadership training holistic in content *and* context?
- What learning environment is missing?
- Do you have a strategy for each learning environment? What is each space for?
- What are the essentials that need to be clearly articulated and taught to every leader?

APPENDIX II: DEVELOPING LEADERS WITH A PLAN

Leadership development is something everyone is committed to but struggles with in the course of life. Sometimes we get motivated and put together a long stream of classes we want leaders to do and call that "development." Other times, we have a pre-planed one-on-one process to guide people through. Or we gather a group of leaders and grow together for a season.

All of these approaches are useful and we use a mix of these at Bread&Wine. However, one of the best tools we created is the leadership development plan. A leadership development plan helps leaders create for themselves a plan to grow in character, competency, and skill by asking questions and giving the leader space to dream and reflect.

Leaders need to own their development. Below is a template to help leaders create a plan. This is their agenda for growth. As a coach, you can use this tool to help them move forward in their big picture goals for their community *and* their own growth.

LEADERSHIP DEVELOPMENT PLAN
Picture of Health

Get with your co-leaders or leaders in training to think through this first section together.

A gospel community exists because of the gospel. We are growing up into a deeper understanding and application of the gospel. We are taking the gospel to the neighborhood, city, and world through intentional missional engagement.

- What would your missional community look like if it was thriving?
- What would your neighborhood look like if it knew Jesus?

- What would it take for them to see the transformation Jesus brings to a community of people?
- What would you like to see happen this year in your missional community?
- What are some goals for your community this year?
- What are a few steps your missional community could take toward your vision?

Leading a Missional Community

In light of those hopes, dreams, and goals, use this section to explore what your role is in leading this missional community.

- What is your role in leading your missional community? How do you think God might use your specific gifts, talents, and story to lead this missional community?
- What isn't your role in leading your missional community? What responsibilities aren't yours?

PERSONAL GROWTH

Leaders are examples in communities of people who are walking in repentance and faith. They are growing in their knowledge of the gospel, belief in the gospel, and obedience to the gospel. One helpful way to think about this transformation is in terms of our head, heart, and hands being conformed to the image of Christ. As you work through this section, look for themes and connections across each area.

Head: Growing in Knowledge

"And do not be conformed to this world, but be transformed by the renewing of your mind, so that you may prove what the will of God is, that which is good and acceptable and perfect." – Romans 12:2

- Where do you need to grow in knowledge?
- Are there things you need to know?
- Is there an issue you need to press into, an issue of Scripture to grow in deeper understanding of?

- Are there pieces of theology you need to learn?
- Are there aspects of gospel communities on mission that you still need to know?
- How will you learn? (i.e. Is there a book or article to read, equipping session you need to attend, commentaries to read, or studies to do, Scripture to memorize, etc.?)

Heart: Growing in Belief

"I pray that the eyes of your heart may be enlightened, so that you will know what is the hope of His calling, what are the riches of the glory of His inheritance in the saints." – Ephesians 1:18

- What areas of life do you need to grow in belief in the gospel?
- What areas do you need to see repentance in?
- What bondage are you volunteering for in your heart? What forgiveness needs to happen?
- How will you grow in belief? (i.e. shepherding conversations to have, questions and issues to bring up in discipleship and accountability groups, what material do you need to walk through, prayer, fasting, retreats, etc.?)

Hands: Growing in Obedience, Skill, and Practice

"Teaching them to obey everything I have commanded." – Matthew 28:20

"Being no hearer who forgets but a doer who acts." – James 1:22-25

"Jesus glorified the Father by accomplishing the work he gave him to do." – John 17:4

- What skills do you need practice in?
- Where are you excelling and in what do you need to keep growing?
- Where are you failing to live what you believe? What skills do you need to develop?
- What thing is God calling you to that requires you to step into in obedience?
- How will you grow in obedience, skill, and practice? (i.e. Are there trainings to attend, do you need to shadow someone, do you need to make a schedule, schedule some specific coaching to help you, are there opportunities for practice and feedback you need to pursue?)

USING THIS TOOL IN COACHING

You can use this tool in a variety of ways in a coaching relationship. It lays the foundation for the entire relationship by giving the coach the leaders's vision for their missional community, their perceived role, and their desires to grow and knowledge of how to grow. It also gives an agenda for subsequent conversations. One can simply sit down to ask: What part of your development plan would you want to talk about today?

This can set a pattern for coaching. I like to use one session to talk about their missional community and learn what one thing the leader could do next to move their community toward their vision. I then set aside the following session to discuss only their development and help them come to next steps in growing as a follower of Christ. This back and forth creates a balance of focusing on the leader and their community.

APPENDIX III: EXAMPLE OF A MISSIONAL COMMITMENT

ALLANDALE/CRESTVIEW MISSIONAL COMMUNITY

By Gods grace we are a missional community in the Allandale/Crestview neighborhood. Because of the gospel of Jesus we want to grow in our devotion to him, to one another, and to our neighbors and city.

Devotion to Jesus

By Gods grace we commit to growing in our devotion to Jesus by:
- Read Paul E. Miller's *The Praying Life* together and discuss.
- Memorize Isaiah 55.
- Learn how to do communal confession together

Devotion to One Another

By Gods grace we commit to growing in our devotion to one another by:
- Having a monthly "Sunday Night Family Dinner" together. Also, open to friends and neighbors. (Organized by X).
- The men in our group will regularly check on single mom to see how we can help her as a single mother. (i.e. yard work, heavy lifting, etc).
- Faithfully encourage X through his battle with cancer through prayer, regular visits, and providing meals via a care calendar.

Devotion to Our Neighbor and City

By Gods grace we commit to growing in our devotion to our neighbors and city together in the Allandale/Crestview neighborhoods, in particular, Gullet Elementary and Lamar Middle School.

- We plan to regularly be present and to serve at the local schools: specifically painting the parent resource room at Lamar Middle School, volunteering at the LamarFest, sponsoring the end of year sports banquet, and pursuing other opportunities to serve the community. X will organize the serve opportunities with the schools since they have kids attending.
- We will regularly pray as a group for our neighbors and friends who do not know and believe the good news of Jesus.
- We will host bi-monthly parties that we intentionally invite our neighbors to.

APPENDIX IV: COACHING CHEAT SHEET

COACHING MINDSET
- Trust the leader to care and lead
- Remember God made them and leads them
- Know your role is a coach in this moment (not consultant, teacher, or shepherd)
- Remember who they are in Christ

A COACHING CONVERSATION MODEL
- Pray to prepare.
- Where are you? What is going on?
- Where are you and your Missional Community headed?
- Where are we headed today? What are some things we need to talk about?
- What is next?
- What can be done about it?
- What will you do about it? When will you do it? What do you need to do that? How can I help?
- Pray!

COACHING SKILLS
- Listening
- Offering Observations
- Speaking Encouragement
- Delivering Clear and Concise Messages
- Resourcing
- Praying and Relying on the Holy Spirit

APPENDIX V: LEADER'S ROLE DESCRIPTION

QUALIFICATIONS OF A LEADER
- Motivated by the gospel.
- Have a desire to help others grow in faith and obedience by pointing them to Jesus.
- Committed to the long process of helping others grow in faith and obedience.
- Prayerful and dependent on God. The Holy Spirit dwells within you. God is your helper that empowers you to love others. Leaders are those who pray and listen to the Spirit.
- Servants to Jesus as Lord. You are selflessly serving Jesus.
- Honest with their own mess as they repent and believe the gospel.
- Understands they can't make people change. Leaders are faithful in sharing the gospel and trying new things, they are also quick to turn to God in prayer and learn from others.
- Submitted to elders of the church.

PRACTICES OF A LEADER
As a leader, you will point people to the gospel in the Bible, speak the gospel in your own words, connect the gospel to people's stories, pray in light of the gospel, and call people to serve as demonstrations of the gospel. Leaders create an environment where community can happen.
- Pray for each individual in in your community.
- Process and think through the state of your community (this can happen in coaching, too).

- Regularly ask how your people are doing as individuals and families? How are you all doing together?
- Regularly pray and ask yourself what it looks like for your community to walk in repentance and faith? What does obedience look like for us? What is God calling us to?
- Share leadership. This means they trust others to lead in specific ways and makes times to get with the other leaders to process and plan.
- Regularly attends leadership huddles and retreats where they share in the learnings of other leaders.
- Connected to a coach who cares for them and helps them process all of the above.

TIME COMMITMENT OF A LEADER

Roughly two hours a week, outside your participation in the missional community you lead.

- One hour praying and processing. As you will likely see a lot of time is spent thinking about and praying for the people in your community. You are also asked to think about the current state of your community and where God is leading you forward.
- One hour preparing or planning. This might mean preparing for discussions, planning meetings, planning missional engagement, etc. This will also likely look like time with coaches and leadership meetings.

APPENDIX VI: MISSIONAL COMMUNITY CHEAT SHEET

THREE PURSUITS OF EVERY MISSIONAL COMMUNITY:

A missional community has three equal and codependent pursuits:

- Grow in Our love for God (Gospel Enjoyment)
- Grow in our love for one-another (Community)
- Grow in our love to our neighbors and city (Mission)

COMMUNITY ISN'T ABOUT YOU

- A Social Club – centered on your relational and social needs.
- A Counseling Group – centered on your emotional needs.
- A Social Service Group – centered on your need to change the world.
- A Neighborhood Association – centered on your neighborhood.
- An Affinity Group – centered on your stage of life and preferences.
- An Event or Meeting – centered on a convenient time-slot.

THE ONE ANOTHER'S OF THE NEW TESTAMENT

- Comfort one-another (2 Cor. 13:11)
- Agree with one-another (2 Cor. 13:11)
- Live in peace with one-another (2 Cor. 13:11)
- Greet one-another (2 Cor. 13:11)

- Bear one-another's burdens—which in context refers to confronting sin and being burdened for the sinful brother (Gal. 6:2)
- Bear with one-another (Eph. 4:2)
- Encourage and build up one-another (1 Thess. 5:11)
- Do not grumble against one-another (Jas. 5:9)
- Do not speak evil against one-another (Jas. 4:11)

APPENDIX VII COMMON MISSION CHEAT SHEET

A common mission is your community's unified effort to love—through word and deed—a specific group of people. As you set out to start and lead a missional community, one of the first things you have to think about is: what will our common mission be. Three broad categories for common missions exist: geographic, network, and marginalized.

- A Neighborhood or Geographic Centric (i.e. ,your town, subdivision, etc.)
- A Network or Affinity Group (i.e., artists, musicians, runners, architects)
- A Marginalized People (i.e., orphans, widows, refugees, captives)

UNDERSTANDING AND CARING ABOUT THE MISSION

Here are five sets of questions to help you move forward in discipling others as a community with the gospel.

- People Questions – Who are the people God is sending us to? Where do they live and hang out? What are their stories? What are their names? What are the avenues to engage and build relationships?
- Language Questions – What "language" do they speak? Are these people young families, business professionals, working class, etc? Rural folks or City people?
- Value Questions – What is most important to them? Success, money, relationships, independence, survival, comfort, escape, etc? Who speaks into their worldview?
- Gospel Questions – What false gospel do they believe in? In other words, what do they hope for? What is the "problem" in their eyes? What is the solution? How is

the gospel good news to them? How does it address their values? How is the gospel better than what they value most right now?

- Needs Questions – What are their needs? How does Jesus meet those needs? How can we be part of meeting their needs in a way that "shows" the gospel?

APPENDIX VIII: ANOTHER MODEL THE "HOUR GLASS"

This traditional coaching model highlights the intentionality and focusing of coaching conversations. It is a helpful picture to have in our heads as coaches because it helps a leader move from broad range of issues to a specific focus on one important thing. As a leader makes decisions, the conversation moves outward to see the impact on the broad issues at the beginning.

CONNECT
Each conversation begins with a relational connection and an initial discovery of some of the issues or opportunities that can be discussed in the conversation. It is in this realm that every potential topic gets put on the proverbial table.

FOCUS
With all the potential topics on the table, a coach facilitates focus towards the one thing. The one important thing to take steps with is not obvious, and it isn't always the most urgent.

DISCOVER
After a focus for the conversation is chosen, the coach and leader work to discover and examine the different factors and aspects of that issue. What makes it hard? How is this related to the whole? What are the barriers? What are the openings? What causes this to surface as something you want to talk about? If this changes, what else changes? What are some things that could be done about it? What are some potential next steps?

ACTION

This processes of focusing and discovering is drawing the conversation to a climatic resolution. What will I do next? When will I do it? How do I need to prepare to do it?

DISCOVER AGAIN AND EVALUATE

Now we get to discover and evaluate the choice. How do we feel about it? How will this next step impact other things? How limited is this next step? What other things might need to be done in follow up? How committed am I to the next step?

APPENDIX IX: ANOTHER MODEL: THE "5 RS"

Robert Logan's, coaching model, mentality, and tools have been very influential on me. This model is excellent. It is easy to remember, easy to implement, and easy to know where you are in the conversation. The 5 Rs give dignity to the leader, the process, and listening to what God is saying and doing. It is also self-explanatory!

RELATE
- How are you?
- What can we celebrate?

REFLECT
- What progress has been made?
- What challenges are you facing?
- Where are you now?
- Where do you sense God wanting you to go?

REFOCUS
- What would be different?
- What are some possible next steps to getting there?
- Which ones seem most helpful for giving you traction to move forward?
- What will you do?

RESOURCE
- Who can come alongside you to help?
- What else do you need?

REVIEW
- What are the next steps you can take between now and our next session?
- What was helpful to you in this conversation?

FURTHER READING AND LEARNING

If you want to dive deeper into coaching philosophy, models, and leadership development, here are some great reads. Some are very corporate and secular while others are theological and Christ-centered.

- *Christ-Centered Coaching* by Jane Creswell
- *Coaching 101* by Robert Logan
- *Co-active Coaching* by Karen and Henry Kimsey-House
- *Fathering Leaders, Motivating Mission* by David Devenish
- *Leverage Your Best and Ditch the Rest* by Scott Blanchard and Madeleine Homan
- *The One Minute Manager* by Ken Blanchard
- *Practicing Affirmation* by Sam Crabtree
- *StrengthsFinder* 2.0 by Tom Rath
- *The Trellis and The Vine* by Collin Marshall and Tony Payne

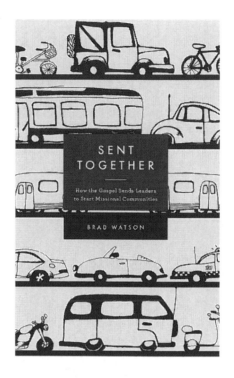

Jesus does not simply call us to be a lovely community together, but he sends us out to our neighborhoods, towns, and cities to declare and demonstrate the gospel. In fact, the gospel beckons men and women to take up the call of leading and starting communities that are sent like Jesus.

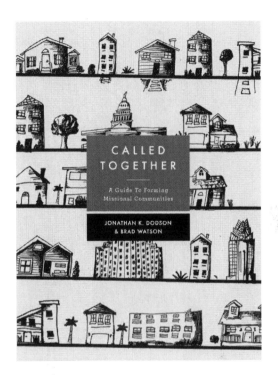

This eight week guide helps communities discover their calling to be and make disciples together. The eight weeks covers important discussions on the gospel, community, and mission while also giving communities next steps to practice what they've talked about.

ABOUT THE AUTHOR

Brad Watson (M.A. in Theology) serves as a pastor at Bread&Wine Communities in Portland, OR. As a member of the planting team, Brad has helped coach, train, and start missional communities throughout the city. One of his greatest passions is helping leaders realize the dreams and calling God has given them for community and mission.

Brad is a regular contributor at WeAreSoma.com, TheVergeNetwork.com, and GospelCenteredDiscipleship.com. He is also co-author of *Raised? Finding Jesus by Doubting the Resurrection* (Zondervan 2014) and *Called Together: A Guide to Forming Missional Communities* (GCD Books 2014).

Brad lives in inner southeast Portland with his wife, Mirela, and their two daughters.

You can read more of his work at bradawatson.com and download free resources for missional communities leaders,and coaching at senttogether.org.

OTHER GCD RESOURCES

Visit GCDiscipleship.com

Small Town Mission is a practical guide for gospel-centered mission in small towns. If you haven't noticed, people who live in small towns have limited options for restaurants, shopping, and books about mission. Small towns desperately need normal, everyday people like farmers, factory workers, teachers, secretaries, and small business owners who think and act like missionaries to reach their friends, neighbors, co-workers, and extended families for Christ. This book aims to help local churches in small towns do that. After all, mission isn't just something that must be prioritized globally and in big cities; it must also be prioritized locally and in small towns.

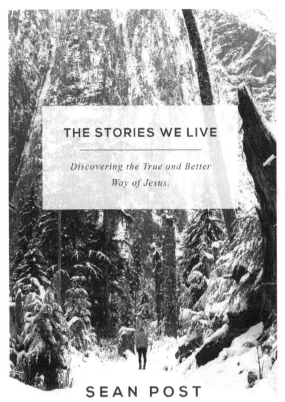

THE STORIES WE LIVE

Discovering the True and Better
Way of Jesus.

SEAN POST

Foreword by RICK MCKINLEY

"The Bible as a whole is a story, a grand narrative, that grips our hearts, our minds, our imaginations. We join with Jesus and His community on a quest which demands our best effort in the team's mission. The end is glorious indeed. *The Stories We Live* is a great introduction to that grand narrative and also some of the broken stories which distract many. Read, be gripped by the story, and join the quest!"

Gerry Breshears, Professor of Theology,
Western Seminary, Portland, OR

Make, Mature, Multiply aims to help you become a disciple who truly understands the full joy of following Jesus. With a wide range of chapters from some of today's most battle-tested disciple-makers, this book is designed for any Christian seeking to know more about being a fully-formed disciple of Jesus who makes, matures, and multiplies fully-formed disciples of Jesus.

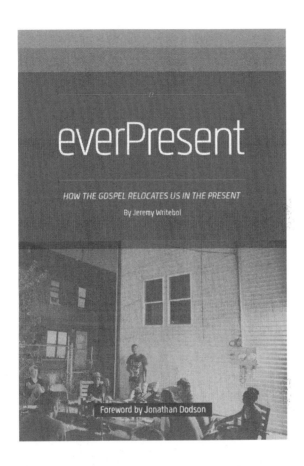

everPresent

HOW THE GOSPEL RELOCATES US IN THE PRESENT

By Jeremy Writebol

Foreword by Jonathan Dodson

"*everPresent* does something that most books don't achieve. Most focus either on who God is or what we should do. Jeremy starts with who God is to walk the reader down the path of what God has done, who we are because of God, then points us to understand what we do because of this. I highly recommend picking up *everPresent* to better understand the why and how of the life of those that follow Jesus."

Seth McBee, Executive Team Member, GCM Collective

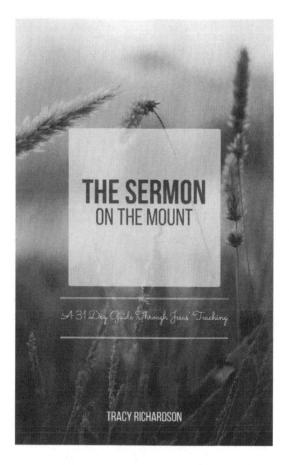

THE SERMON
ON THE MOUNT

A 31 Day Guide Through Jesus' Teaching

TRACY RICHARDSON

In *The Sermon on the Mount: A 31 Day Guide Through Jesus' Teaching*, Tracy Richardson walks us through Jesus' teaching in hopes that the Spirit will transform the hearts of his disciples. This guide is designed specifically for DNA groups, two to three people, who meet weekly under the leadership of the Spirit.